Cooked to Perfection

How to respond when life turns up the heat

D0167443

Elizabeth Cody Newenhuyse

ZondervanPublishingHouse

Grand Rapids, Michigan

A Division of HarperCollins*Publishers*

Cooked to Perfection
Copyright © 1997 by Elizabeth Cody Newenhuyse

Requests for information should be addressed to:

📖ZondervanPublishingHouse
Grand Rapids, Michigan 49530

Library of Congress Cataloging-in-Publication Data

Newenhuyse, Elizabeth Cody.
    Cooked to perfection: how to respond when life turns up the heat /
Elizabeth Cody Newenhuyse.
        p. cm.
        ISBN: 0-310-20163-2
    1. Suffering—Religious aspect—Christianity. 2. Newenhuyse, Elizabeth
Cody. I. Title.
BV4909.N48 1997
248.8'6–dc 21   97-26779
                                                                              CIP

Interior design by Jody A. DeNeef

Printed in the United States of America

---

97 98 99 00 01 02 03 04 /❖ DC/ 10 9 8 7 6 5 4 3 2 1

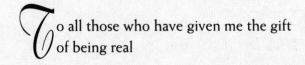
To all those who have given me the gift
of being real

Contents

Suffering Hurts . . . So What Good Is It? . . . 7

Chapter One
The Time I Turned Orange, and Other Tales of Grace . . .15

Chapter Two
Why We Tell Childbirth Stories 25

Chapter Three
Living Beyond Our Limits 35

Chapter Four
I Cried Till I Laughed 45

Chapter Five
Hey, Did You Hear the One About the Leaky Roof? 55

Chapter Six
Walking by Faith . . . Toward What? 65

Chapter Seven
Surprise! God Showed Up! 77

Chapter Eight
Have Mercy! 89

Chapter Nine
Angels and Kids and Mismatched Chairs 99

Chapter Ten
Not "Why" But "Who" 109

Chapter Eleven
Morning by Morning, New Mercies 121

Acknowledgments

What if roles were reversed and there was one sheep with many shepherds? That's how I've felt bringing this book to life, as if I've had many wise, gentle, sometimes challenging shepherds. Jack Kuhatschek led me through the process with deft editorial guidance. Pastor John Benson came alongside with spiritual wisdom and support. My precious friends Diane Eble, Eileen Silva Kindig, and Barbara Tennyson walked me up the peaks and down the valleys, while my family—husband Fritz, daughter Amanda, and mother Beverly—were there with love and belief.

I also want to acknowledge my gratitude to Bruce Zabel, my longtime agent who is leaving the field for other publishing pastures. Bruce worked with integrity and vision and a commitment to authors; his presence will be missed in our publishing community.

Finally, a note about the biblical texts quoted herein. I've drawn extensively on two newer Bibles: *The Message*, Eugene Peterson's fresh and vivid paraphrase of the New Testament, and *The Quest Study Bible*, which tackles many of the tough "Why-would-God-say-*that*?" questions many Christians ask. I've found both treatments indispensable in helping to illuminate God's Word.

To God alone be the glory.

Suffering Hurts ... So What Good Is It?

In a way, it's proof of God's sense of humor that you're holding this book in your hands. When the good people at Zondervan first asked me if I would be interested in writing a book on how God uses our struggles and weaknesses to bring growth and transformation—in effect, the "gifts" that hard times can yield—I thought, *But what do I say? I don't like pain or even minor annoyances. When I shower, I'm so afraid of getting shampoo in my eyes that I wear industrial safety glasses.*

Okay, just kidding. But I've been known to go to, well, unusual lengths to protect myself. When I was a kid we lived in a new house surrounded by open fields. It was great growing up in a rural ambiance, but we paid a price—in rainy summers, hordes of mosquitoes would descend like the Visigoths sacking Rome, and at least half of them, it seemed, made their way into the house. Once, when I was about eight, I remember a mosquito whining around my head one night as I tried to sleep. Actually, it sounded like a Vienna Boys' Choir of mosquitoes. I could have bravely turned on the light, hunted the beast(s) down, and dispatched them. But I did not want to be brave; I wanted to be comfortable. I went into the bathroom, closed the door, and lay down on the floor, where I dozed fitfully the entire night.

So now—to write a book about suffering, and how suffering may even be good for you? Been there, done that. I've *lived*

suffering. Suffering hurts. I'd rather write something funny—
"101 Excuses for a Cinnamon-Bun Run," for example.

Okay, God, What Are You Doing?

I've tried for years to understand some things, and in
the process, I've become really annoyed with God on
behalf of people I care about: *Okay, Lord, first her husband
couldn't find a job and now she has a lump in her breast. That's just
great, God.* I've wanted, Habakkuk-like, to challenge God.

Well, God doesn't seem to mind being challenged. For
one thing, he's God. He can take it. But also, I believe, if
we're honestly questioning him, it means we're seeking to
move closer to him, like the psalmist who says, "I believed;
therefore I said, 'I am greatly afflicted'" (116:10).

Boy—afflictions. Who doesn't have them? As I was
wrestling with this book, several of my dearest friends were
wrestling with their own troubles. Health problems.
Money worries. Discouragement over where their lives
were going. The expression "I feel your pain" has become a
cliché, but I did: I felt their pain, and I began to wonder
about the purpose for that pain. One friend said, in a
moment of candor, "Don't just quote Romans 8:28 at me
and leave it at that." The fingerprints of my friends' struggles, of their courage and grace, are all through this book.

It has seemed to me that many of the books that seek to
make sense out of pain either dwell too much on the darkness or are in a hurry to get to the sunshine. One attitude
says, "Life is tough, we live in a fallen world, and misery is
our lot." And the other attitude is well expressed by Becky
Pippert in her book *Hope Has Its Reasons*:

> I have one friend who comes across as so spiritual he
> never seems to have a bad day. . . . One time he came
> striding in triumphantly and said, "Hello, Becky. Praise

God! How are you? The Lord is good! My car was totaled. Thank you, Jesus!"

"Yes, yes," I said, rather routinely. "Everything is fine . . . *What did you just say?*"

"God is good," he replied.

"I got that part. But what about your car?"

"It was totaled last night. Praise the Lord!" he answered with a glow.

I was shocked. "But that's *terrible!*" I exclaimed.

"Not when you know the Lord!" he retorted. And off he went on an apparent celestial cloud.

Becky goes on to muse about the tensions believers face. Does trusting God and living in the Spirit mean that somehow problems just disappear? Or (my words, not hers) does being saved mean that we're supposed to live in a sort of weird, parallel universe where human feelings are repressed and such nuisances as wrecked cars are occasions for going around in a happy glow?

Not Us, but God

Well, no. And yet—I'm talking as much to myself as to you—we can't get so cynical and fatalistic that we're blinded to God's grace, God's surprises, God's working in everyone and everything according to his purpose.

Anyway, as I pondered what to say in this book, I began to agonize over the need to be honest *and* hopeful, realistic *and* encouraging. I wrote revision after revision. It got to the point where nearly everyone I knew started cracking jokes like, "Oh, you're suffering through the suffering book." Ha ha, very funny.

But as I completed the final chapters, I realized that, while this is indeed a book about hope in the midst of struggle, it is more than that. It's a book about *God* and how hard times can reveal his working in us and through us. I like what Oswald Chambers says: "God does not further our spiritual life in spite of our circumstances, but in and by our circumstances. The whole purpose of God is to make the ideal faith actually real in the lives of His servants."

As I've depended on Scripture to reveal God's truth about suffering, I've been reminded of how that "ideal" becomes actuality. God's Word cannot be reduced to a page-a-day inspirational calendar. There's a wonderfully healing, vigorous, and tough-minded specificity where "it is written." Answers, yes, but often in the form of stories of real people with real pain: I found Paul begging God three times to remove his thorn; Elijah lying down under the broom tree to go to sleep; David weeping for his son; Moses lamenting to God that he was sick of listening to the people complain; Jacob dislocating his hip in a wrestling match with an angel. And finally, Jesus himself, near his earthly completion, looking at his sleeping friends and wondering why they weren't there for him in his hour of need.

Every one of these lives—including the Life himself— points us toward God. If we open ourselves up to his work in us, everything that happens in our lives can bring us closer to him. We are "more than conquerors," but not, perhaps, in the way we usually think. The victory is found in the way God *redeems* our struggles. He is with each of us, he has called us by name (Isa. 43), and he can and will *use* us to his glory.

If you take away one thing from this book, I hope it is amazement at how God can use our wonderful muddle of humanness to accomplish his purposes. He doesn't care if we haven't solved everything or if we're crybabies at times. In fact, I think he may prefer it that way, because the broken parts of ourselves give him cracks to enter into our hearts.

Consider the Crocus

I'm looking out at my yard as I write this. The wind is blowing like crazy, banging a handpainted "Welcome to Our Home" plaque against the side of our front porch. (This is one reason I'm glad I'm a woman and not a man: I woke my husband, Fritz, at three this morning with, "Honey, that banging is keeping me awake. Could you go outside and . . . ?" After the requisite bit of grumbling, he manfully put on his robe and slippers and ventured out into the icy blackness so that his beloved could get her beauty sleep. I wish he'd been around when that mosquito was making my life miserable thirty-some years ago!) It's that indeterminate time between late winter and early spring; a few brave crocus shoots are pushing up through the ground in the sheltered places while little spits of snow flurries swirl around them. Last Sunday it was warm, a lot warmer than today, and we heard one very premature overachieving robin singing in a yard near our church. In this case, I'd say the early bird doesn't catch the worm, he catches double pneumonia.

You may be hurting right now, and with this book, I want to give you crocuses blooming amid the flurries. They may not be as showy as their daffodil cousins, but they're tougher. A warm spell will bring them out, but a cold snap won't batter them down. Not only that, but they can pop up in unexpected places, like the middle of a lawn, and do just fine.

And so will you, if you unfold yourself to God's care and tending.

Learning from the Lindberghs

After my father passed away a few years ago, a friend (who herself lost her dad when she was only a teenager) gave me a little book on loss and suffering by Anne Morrow Lindbergh, a gifted writer and the wife of the famous aviator Charles Lindbergh. Charles Lindbergh, of course, was the first pilot to cross the Atlantic, in 1927. Immediately he was lionized as an authentic American hero. It was an era of larger-than-life celebrities—baseball player Babe Ruth, boxer Jack Dempsey, glamorous Hollywood stars—and the spotlight shone mercilessly on the shy Lindbergh and his young wife. They did their best to retreat from its glare, but in 1932 they were once again in the news as victims of what was called "the crime of the century"—the kidnapping of their eighteen-month-old baby. Somehow, someone climbed a ladder into their New Jersey home and grabbed the boy out of his crib, leaving a ransom note. The ransom was paid, but the baby's body was found ten weeks later.

I've often thought there must be a peculiarly awful sort of horror in having your child abducted. To think that your precious little one, whom you have always tried to keep safe, is *out there* somewhere, alone and afraid. Then, to ultimately lose the child, and, in the media hysteria surrounding the case, be denied the dignity of private grieving . . . I cannot imagine. Anne Lindbergh went through the fire, and many years later, tried to draw some perspective from it all. One of her observations struck me as right on target: "I do not believe that suffering alone teaches. If suffering alone taught, all the world would be wise, since everyone suffers. To suffering must be added mourning, understanding, patience, love, openness, and the willingness to remain vulnerable."

We Would See Jesus . . .

To Anne Morrow Lindbergh's words I would add one thing—the willingness to fling our laughter into the face of the Liar, because Satan doesn't get the joke. He doesn't understand honest and healing humor.

Even in the midst of our muddles, we must remember the joy. Erika Carney, a woman involved in urban ministry in Chicago, wrote in the North Park College student newspaper about all the hopelessness she had encountered as she dealt with inner-city youth. It had thrust her into a real crisis of faith. "In my mind," she writes, "all that was good became an escape, or a false reality that I could no longer be deceived by." She finally realized something very important: "If I am going to watch Jesus die, it is crucial that I am also able to see Jesus live."

We can see Jesus live when we feel deeply, laugh loudly, cry unashamedly, learn daily—and when we are able to share these feelings and lessons with others. We can see Jesus live *in us* as we come to realize that we are being refined into creatures reflecting a bit of the glory of the Creator—through our struggles and suffering.

The Butterball Conquest

Here's another confession (you'll find quite a few of them throughout this book). I didn't cook my first Thanksgiving turkey until I was about forty. Never had to; we always went to my parents'. Besides, I imagined roasting a turkey was something incredibly difficult and mysterious. I had watched my mother checking and basting and checking and basting and doing things with foil. My husband once won a frozen turkey in some raffle, and it sat in our freezer for a year until I finally gave it to my mother-in-law.

But turning forty has that watershed feeling that spurs you to accomplish all sorts of goals. I lost weight, published my first book, *and* decided I was being ridiculous about this turkey business. After all, I was and am a good cook. So I told my mother we would be staying home for Thanksgiving. We then went to the supermarket and picked up a Butterball—and the worry started. Would it defrost in time for the feast? Did I use a shallow or deep roaster? What about making the stuffing? Should I truss? How would I know when it was done? And then the gravy . . .

Thanksgiving arrived. I got up before everyone else, made the dressing, prepared the bird, and shoved it into the oven with the feeling of having crossed a Rubicon. Then the anxious waiting started. Hours later—but not as many hours as I would have guessed—the familiar, wonderful fragrance began to permeate the house. It was working! Finally I peeked in the oven. It smelled done. It looked done.

It was. It looked like a Norman Rockwell turkey—golden-brown, moist, oozing stuffing. It tasted even better than some of my mother's turkeys. It really *was* cooked to perfection. All the sweat and perseverance had paid off. Having a little faith in myself had paid off. Reading the directions had paid off.

And so it is with growth through struggle. We will pass through the fire, but the flames will not consume us. We have God's promise on that. And then, as we persevere, take the risk of growth, and read the "directions"—God's Word—we come out the other side. Cooked to perfection. Not "perfection" as we understand it in worldly terms, but *being perfected* through our trials. Wiser. More merciful. More patient. More loving. More trusting. More willing to risk. More aware of the bigness and wonderfulness of God.

Believe it. Trust it. Live it.

And so let's reach out to one another with our scarred hands. Let's go, together, to see Jesus live.

Chapter One

The Time I Turned Orange, and Other Tales of Grace

The following story has never seen the light of print until now. Not even my best friends know about it. Nobody has ever heard the tale except my husband and my family of origin, and I hope that even they have mercifully blocked it out of their memories. I tell it to you now because it will help you understand a little about me, what I've gone through, and what God has shown me.

It was the spring of 1965, and I was in high school. I wanted to fit in, be popular, be noticed.

I did not fit in.

Let's just say that out of a student body of nearly five thousand strong, I was a cipher, a nobody. I had attended a small grade school, kindergarten through eighth, where everybody knew everybody else. I participated in Girl Scouts and after-school sports, and I got fairly good grades. But it's really hard to go from a graduating class of eighty-five to a freshman class the size of a small college. Especially when you tend to be shy and awkward anyway. Not only that, but this high school was, and is, located in what is probably one of the most affluent and high-achieving communities in the country. The school has produced corporate titans, U.S. senators, network news reporters, NFL stars, eminent physicians, best-selling authors, and even a fair number of Hollywood types. So the pressure to be popular and successful is even more grinding. (Let the record show, however, that some of these adult achievers hardly show up in their school yearbooks. Ha!)

Well, anyway, this spring of 1965, the "in" look was the surfer image—blond, tan. You may remember the model Cheryl Tiegs. Her look typified the era: straight bleached hair, lots of eyeliner, golden skin. I had the blonde hair, but it was too thick and curly, even after I punished myself every night by sleeping on rollers the size of industrial drums. I had the eyeliner, but before I got contacts, it was hidden behind thick glasses.

What I needed, I decided, was the tan.

Nobody worried about the dangers of the sun back then, so some days I would lie out in it for hours on end like a Boston Market chicken, grilling on the rotisserie. Still, I couldn't quite achieve that sun-bunny effect.

Lucky for me, instant-tanning solutions had just appeared on the market. Before-and-after ads showed pasty-white people achieving tans worthy of George Hamilton, that suave actor who always boasts a coppery sheen. So I convinced my mother to get me some (as the parent of a middle-school child now, I wonder that she was an accessory to my fecklessness), and one night I slathered it on, anticipating my transformation into a true surfer girl. *Now* I would get noticed.

I did. But, unfortunately, not because of my stunning tan.

The products, being new, had not, shall we say, been perfected. I awoke the next day, peered at my skin, and shrieked. It looked as if I had a bad case of jaundice. The "golden tan" promised was more of a sickly orange. Worse, in the places where I had applied it most heavily, dark patches made me look as if I had some kind of melanin imbalance.

I tried to scrub it off, to no avail. I begged my mother to let me stay home from school, to no avail. So off I went to endure a day of finger-pointing and snickering. I wanted to sink through the floor. This was not new; even on *good* days, I had intense moments of wanting to sink through the floor in an agony of adolescent self-consciousness. But on this day I wanted to sink all the way to some mythical Pacific island where my pigmentation would fit in with the native populace.

And I had only wanted to fit in.

The "tanning solution" wasn't permanent, thank goodness. It wore off. But my adolescent desire to fit in did not. Another time—hey, I'm on a roll; I might as well confess to other abject humiliations—I wore a paper dress to school. This isn't as weird as it sounds. I think there was an article in *Seventeen* magazine about paper dresses being the new fad, and readers could actually find one folded inside the pages. The material resembled a sturdy paper towel. The novelty appealed to me; so once again, off I went to school, this time wearing the equivalent of Quilted Bounty.

Well, since the sixties, tanning potions have been perfected, but paper dresses never caught on—and there's a good reason. Short of clothing one's body in one of those cushioned book mailers, paper does not stand up to human wear and tear—as in sitting, standing, walking, and sweating. By the end of the school day, my dress was riddled with slits. This time I wanted to vanish off the face of the earth.

The Embarrassing Teen Within

I look back now and wonder, *What planet was I on? What in the world was I thinking?* Today I'm prudent, semi-appearance-conscious, and not in the least flamboyant. I don't do much without thinking it through carefully. But somewhere inside, that lonely teenager remains. Every now and then, I dream at night that I desperately want to be friends with some group, only to be cruelly rejected. Every now and then, even in my mid-forties, I feel a sense of awkward bashfulness in certain groups where everyone else seems to be having fun. There she is again, that overeager teenager, crashing the party like an embarrassing relative who doesn't get invited to family gatherings because she might get drunk or tell silly stories for the hundredth time.

For a long time, I wanted nothing to do with her. I just wanted to get away from my suffering. Like Scarlett O'Hara, I vowed: "As God is my witness, I'll never be unsuccessful again!"

After high school, I went away to a very small college where I made friends and actually became something of a campus leader. Shortly after college I became a Christian. And then God led me to the church singles group where I met the man who would become my husband. In one of God's great ironies, Fritz, who was two years ahead of me in high school, was Mr. Everything—football and track star, an officer in the all-school boys' club, president of the local Young Life chapter, accepted at Harvard, Yale, and Princeton. I knew who he was. He did not know who I was. We sometimes have conversations now that resemble cross-cultural exchanges. Me: "So, tell me. What was it like to be popular?" He: "Honestly, we hardly knew people like you existed."

We married, served in a pastorate for a number of years, became parents, bought a house, grew together in our Christian life. I began to achieve some career goals. We became involved in a church we love, connected with like-souled friends, watched our daughter grow into a dear and special little person.

It took me a long time to *get it*—that God meant to use my adolescent pain. I preferred to focus on what was good and successful and positive in my life. Even within the Christian community, I admired strength, not weakness; achievement, not failure; acclamation, not obscurity. I wanted to identify with those "successful" believers and build a brick wall between myself and that silly adolescent with her orange tan and paper dress. I know, it doesn't sound Christlike; it sounds worldly and shallow. But understand this: they *hurt*, those memories. I can laugh about them now, but would I want to go back to high school and relive those experiences? Not on your life.

Taking Our Failures Out of the Closet

I'm beginning to see that God works most powerfully through our pain, through our weakness, through those failures and embarrassments that we would rather not admit to. We can hide nothing from God; he knows everything, and he wants us to lay bare every part of our lives to him, including those skeletons in our emotional and spiritual closets.

I really admire minister Bill Hybels. Not so much because of how God has worked through him at the Willow Creek megaministry or because he writes best-selling books or because he is a gifted speaker and Bible teacher. No, I admire Hybels because he can get up before groups like the assemblage at the Moody Bible Institute Founders' Week celebration and talk about how he sometimes feels out of "spiritual union" with God, and how he writes down his prayers because if he just speaks them he gets distracted. If he simply went up on the platform and dazzled everybody with success stories of the souls saved through Willow Creek—and there are probably thousands of such stories— I would applaud the growth of the Kingdom through his ministry, but a part of me would feel shut out. After all, I can boast of no such achievement. But if *he* struggles with the same kinds of weaknesses as I do, and has found, through opening himself up to God's Spirit, some ways to deal with them, then I know there's hope for me.

And there's hope for you too. If we trust him, God can bring good out of anything, can use anything. I think of the story in John 9 where Jesus restores sight to the blind man. Remember what he put on the man's eyes? Plain old mud. Can't get much more humble and "earthly" than that. The man then went to the pool and washed off the mud, and suddenly he could see Jesus. In the same way, God uses the mud in our lives to bring us to a clearer vision of him and the free gift of grace he holds out for us.

Bald, Blind, and Single?

Paul knew something about visions and blindness. But he chose, instead, to call attention to his weakness. Eugene Peterson's paraphrase is worth sharing at length:

> Because of the extravagance of these revelations, and so I wouldn't get a big head, I was given the gift of a handicap to keep me in constant touch with my limitations. Satan's angel did his best to get me down; what he in fact did was push me to my knees. No danger then of walking around high and mighty! At first I didn't think of it as a gift, and begged God to remove it. Three times I did that, and then he told me, "My grace is enough; it's all you need. My strength comes into its own in your weakness." Once I heard that, I was glad to let it happen. I quit focusing on the handicap and began appreciating the gift. It was a case of Christ's strength moving in my weakness. Now I take limitations in stride, and with good cheer, these limitations that cut me down to size— abuse, accidents, opposition, bad breaks. I just let Christ

take over! And so the weaker I get, the stronger I become
(2 Cor. 12, THE MESSAGE).

We don't know what Paul's handicap or "thorn" was. But
certainly he cut an unprepossessing figure. I like the pithi-
ness of the title of an article about him in *Christian History*
magazine: "Bald, Blind, and Single?" Those who knew the
Apostle only from his letters were possibly disappointed
when meeting him for the first time, the way one might feel
when meeting a pen pal: "His letters are weighty and force-
ful, but in person he is unimpressive" (2 Cor. 10:10).

Homeliness was one thing. But Paul may have spent as
much as a quarter of his ministry in chains, and, reports
Christian History, the conditions in Roman prisons were so
intolerable that "many prisoners begged for a speedy
death." Cells were dark, dank, freezing, and smelly. Impris-
onment was preceded by flogging, and wounds were left
untreated. Prisoners were given little food or water. And
Paul, by the reckoning of the time, was not a young man.

This amazes me. My idea of "roughing it" is going without complimentary soap or shampoo in a hotel bathroom.
When working at my computer, I sigh impatiently if I have
to get up and hunt for a paper clip. To think of this aging
man, perhaps struggling with poor eyesight, wrapped only
in a thin cloak, scratching out a letter in a dim cell while
irons cut into his flesh is incredibly moving. And he wrote
with such wisdom, clarity, and joy. I don't understand it,
and, in not understanding, I'm pulled closer to God, which
is exactly Paul's intention.

It is *not* Paul's intention—in my opinion—that we feel
guilty for complaining about our own circumstances. What
he was saying was: "Look at me, the unlikeliest of commu-
nicators. Look how God is using me. And be strengthened
in *your* pain and weakness."

Paul pulls us away from the sight of the ugly chains and points to the risen Christ, who defeated death. He says, clearly, that suffering is not the end. It's not something to be ashamed of. In Christ, the tables have been turned, the old standards upended. The last is first. The weak are the strong. The barren woman will rejoice. Those who are poor are the blessed.

What's Winning Got to Do with It?

We keep getting this wrong. At least, I know I do. We love winners. Right now, as I write this, my beloved Bulls are on track to win an unbelievable seventy games, which would be an NBA record. But try getting a ticket to a game! (The skyboxes are probably all filled with lawyers who went to my high school.) We may mouth the words, "Better to be faithful than successful," but we lo-o-ove success. We may admire the pastor struggling along in that old brick church on the downtown street corner, but we don't want to go there, not with its funny smell and handful of worshipers and no parking. We would rather drive a ways to the sprawling new "campus" of the church on the outer edge of suburbia, with its spacious narthex and cushy seats and air-conditioning and sanctuary—now called an "auditorium" or "worship center." (Somehow, an invocation that proclaims, "The Lord is in his auditorium; let us worship him together" falls as short as a missed jump shot.)

God sees things differently. It is in those cracks of pain and weakness and need where he works most forcefully, filling the cracks, not with success, but with his grace. He says, "Bring your pain, your need, your struggle to me— and I will make something of it. I will use it to my glory." And he does this both in the bustling megachurch complex—where people *are* suffering, but are good at covering it up—and in the dank old downtown sanctuary.

Back to my adolescent struggles. I don't know that I'd go as far as a woman I know who said, "My wound may be the best part of me," but I know what she was getting at. Our wounds may be the softest and most yielding parts of us, those parts most open to God's working.

Becoming *Real*

As I reflect on my life journey so far, I think that perhaps my pain has given me a deeper sense of gratitude . . . see the connection with *grace?* . . . than I might otherwise have. I do not take things for granted. My husband and I were talking about this the other night. We're in the habit of saying things about our house like, "Don't we have a nice house? Aren't we lucky we live where we do?" It sounds sort of sickening and self-congratulatory, I know. But it isn't intended that way. We're truly grateful for we've both known times when having a house and a family seemed like unattainable dreams. It's a bit like someone who survives a life-threatening heart attack or near-fatal accident and appreciates the gift of life all the more. I once heard Bible teacher Haddon Robinson say that, as an only child who lost his mother at a young age, he was perhaps more grateful for his friends than someone else might be. I can relate. My husband, my daughter, my friends, my church: I don't assume these as a given, but as a gift.

This may be a part of my personality; I tend to be an "appreciator," loving the little, overlooked things like the iridescent blue-green of my parakeet's feathers and the fragrance of crushed garlic as it sautés in olive oil. (I say, forget chocolate and give me olive oil which, by the way, is scriptural. Jesus, as far as we know, did not eat chocolate.)

I also think that I have a deeper compassion for others' suffering, because I, too, have suffered. I dislike smugness and complacency and people who don't seem grateful for what they have. In fact, it really ticks me off. I realize that the people with whom I seem to click have luminous depths, like phosphorescence in tropical seas, that come from really living, really crying, really laughing. Like the Skin Horse in the classic story *The Velveteen Rabbit*, who was battered and torn and so loved, these people are *real*.

God uses everything. Couldn't I have learned some of this an easier way? Couldn't I have become compassionate and grateful and intuitive if I had been popular and if Fritz and I had always had lots of money and if my life had been free of pain?

I'm not sure. This is the portion I was given, and God has his reasons for everything. Yes, I do have regrets. I sometimes regret missing out on what I've heard is the fun of adolescence. I pray that my daughter will be spared some of the pain I had to go through.

But God knows best. He wants me to become *real*. Maybe that embarrassing teenage girl is always with me to remind me of his goodness and power. Or maybe she's there as a reminder not to get too puffed up about myself—sort of the spiritual equivalent of spinach in the teeth. Or perhaps as a way to spark connection with others who have similarly suffered? I don't know. But I believe that these sorrows are, in a sense, a gift: the gift of transformation through struggle, a gift that is available to all of us.

Because if God can use teenage trauma, he can use anything, transform anything—and anyone. He can use you and your struggles and sorrows to his glory, helping you grow in him. I've seen it in my life. What a Lord we serve!

I still don't let anyone see photos of me from my high-school days. But I think I'm finally growing in gratitude for that girl. She's taught me a lot.

Chapter Two

Why We Tell Childbirth Stories

One Sunday, as I taught a marriage class at my church, the subject of communication between husbands and wives came up, and so I began to teach about some of the conditions that foster intimacy. "Husbands do not like to be asked, 'How are you, *really*?'" I said. "If I ask my husband that, he runs into the garage and starts throwing heavy tools around." (Here, the wives started grinning and nudging their husbands.) I then listed some nonthreatening paths to communication and, with a standup comic's flair for the non sequitur, somehow segued into a discussion of how, after you've been married a long time, you hear each other's stories over and over.

"Men, why is it," I wondered aloud, "that every former athlete, whether he was a pro or college or even high school star, remembers the *exact* details of some triumph on the field? 'The count's two and two, one out, man on second, wind blowing toward the fence ...' 'There we are, third and long, when Kowalski hands off the ball to me and I go around the end and ...'" (Note how these tales are always told in the immediacy of the present tense.) Women, I concluded smugly, have no such detailed equivalent.

"Oh yes they do," retorted a veteran husband and father. "Childbirth stories."

And Then He Said, "Push!"

I laughed—because he's right. Women remember *exactly* how long they were in labor, how many centimeters they were dilated when they got to the hospital, what the walls of the room looked like. And, for some reason, they—we—love to regale others with pant-by-blow accounts, although I know some feel that childbirth stories are right up there with warm milk and vacation slides as a soporific.

That said, permit me a quick story of my own experience of labor and delivery. My water broke two hours after we had gone to bed and two weeks before the estimated due date. I'll spare you the minutiae of how I ate a banana on the way to the hospital and how cool it was when we reported to the night emergency entrance and how the nurse called for a wheelchair and two minutes later there it was, and how oddly detached I felt throughout the whole process, as if I were watching myself having a baby. . . . Anyway, the baby kept not coming. (Even then, Amanda was dawdling.) I had to stay in the hospital to guard against infection, but nothing was happening. We waited for eight hours. I heard talk of a C-section, but a nurse finally administered the labor-inducing drug Pitocin.

If I had known then what I know now, I would have reacted like one of those movie victims: "Oh, no! Not that! Anything but that!" With Pit, as it's cheerfully called, there's no gradual warm-up. It's like you go bang, right into transition, the most painful peak of labor. I lay there curled up in a fetal position, moaning, finally giving up on my breathing, wishing everyone would just go away. Thanks to the wonders of medical technology I could observe my agony on the monitor, which graphed a jagged mountain range of contractions like a kindergartner's drawing of the Rockies.

My labor seemed to last forever, but the whole thing, from beginning to end, was probably just a couple of hours. Then, when I was momentarily alone in the birthing room—having driven everyone away with my foul temper—I felt that indescribable urge to push. When the nurse returned to check on me, I said, "Um, something's happening." She looked, gasped, and went into action.

When it was all over there she was, a beautiful, delicate-featured, slightly blood-smeared baby girl. If you're a mother, I don't have to tell you how it feels the first time you lay eyes on your child. They cleaned her up, weighed her, and performed all the other immediate postnatal checking. Then they laid her in my arms. Oh, she was so tiny!

She isn't so tiny anymore. But she still allows me to hold her on my lap sometimes. I love her so much that I feel like the momma rabbit in *The Runaway Bunny*—she can't escape me, ever, because I'll be there to touch and hold her. It makes me wonder if the reason we tell childbirth stories is to testify to the fact that out of the messiest, most prolonged, most painful experiences are born the things that are God's best for us.

Spiders and Sickness and Tears, Oh My!

My friend Diane has two kids, an infant and a preschooler. Between the two of them she isn't getting much sleep. We talked about this for a long time the other day, and finally I said, "You know, Diane, part of it is that having young kids is just *hard*."

I hear often from young moms who have read my book *Sometimes I Feel Like Running Away from Home* and are wondering when they can get their life back. (I don't know how to tell them, "About the time you get excited because there's a two-for-one sale on cellulite cream at Target.") One mom who wrote me had a three-year-old, a one-year-old, and a third on the way. Her three-year-old was going through the throes of potty training, both of her kids kept getting sick, and on top of all that, the family had moved to the South from the Midwest and she discovered that the big yard that had seemed so appealing at first was a convention center for poisonous insects, including black widow spiders.

Yet, as hard and even heartbreaking as it can be to raise children, who among us would trade the experience? I've had times when I feel like a big open vein walking around—and Amanda's a relatively easy child. She mentions a simple little thing like school cliques, and I get really upset and immediately start thinking about the possibilities of home schooling. (It does seem, doesn't it, that other people's children are always the perpetrators of snottiness—never one's own precious bundles?) I worry for her, pray for her, even—greater love hath no mother—try to help her with her math.

The hard thing may be the best thing.

Here again, God turns things upside down. I wouldn't say that he *causes* suffering so we can be "tested." But he does *allow* our faith to be tested so that we may be brought closer to him.

Are We Getting Graded on This?

Peter knew something about being tested. When Jesus asked his disciples, "What are people saying about me? What's the word?" it was Peter who passed the test, responding with his usual alacrity, "You are the Christ!" It was Peter who—no doubt to his great surprise—was enabled to walk on water. (I picture him, a little unsteady, arms held out, glancing down at his feet, wondering, *Is this me?*)

It was Peter who stoutly told the Master, "I won't fail your test, Rabbi. Even though everyone else turns his back on you, I'll be right there." Jesus may have regarded him with a mixture of affection and sadness as he replied, "No, my dear friend. You won't."

Jesus, of course, knew that Peter's lion heart would fail him only temporarily, and that even greater testing lay ahead for him. Peter wrote his letters at a time of increasing Roman persecution of Christians—Peter himself was beaten and imprisoned. He was strengthened through his testing and able to declare to the young church that "these [trials] have come so that your faith—of greater worth than gold, which perishes even though refined by fire—may be proved genuine and may result in praise, glory and honor when Jesus Christ is revealed" (1 Pet. 1:7).

The story of Job takes this even further. It opens with God talking to Satan, extolling Job: "Have you considered my servant Job? There is no one on earth like him" (1:8). The implication is that the Lord thought so highly of Job that he was confident his servant would come through his time of testing with a faith not only unshaken, but stronger than ever.

It's easy to talk about all this in the abstract, of course. If we're honest, we have to admit that when we're actually in the middle of a hard time, our noble intentions to give everything to God can fly out the window. It's kind of like how we determine to go through natural childbirth—no pharmaceutical intervention—until the pain gets unbearable. Then we groan, "Forget the stupid breathing and just give me *drugs!*" We don't need the dubious distinction of being singled out for suffering.

You may be in that place where it seems like the light at the end of the tunnel is always the proverbial oncoming train. One thing seems to be piling on another and you're now checking your skin for boil outbreaks. Can you affirm, at least intellectually, that eventually—maybe not right away, but eventually—some of this will sort itself out? Can you believe God is in control and that the promises of Scripture can be trusted? You may not love it, not at the moment, but can you at least trust God in it?

I Don't Get It, God

When we're blundering through the trees, trying not to trip over roots and deadfalls, it's hard to sense the shape of the whole forest. We're in the midst of something we don't understand. And guess what? That's all right. It's not for *us* to know the forest in its entirety.

God doesn't do things the way we would. We can give lip service to Isaiah 55:9, "As the heavens are higher than the earth, so are my ways higher than your ways and my thoughts than your thoughts," but I suspect that we too often secretly impose our own human templates on how we think God should act. For example, if I were God and wanted to redeem the world, I wouldn't have chosen to preach to a bunch of lowly provincial nobodies. The preferred marketing strategy is to amass a group of influential "gatekeepers," those in a position to reach other large groups, and get them behind you, the way presidential candidates line up party leaders. I would, therefore, have made sure I had the Sanhedrin and the wealthy merchants and landowners in my corner. I wouldn't have spoken Aramaic, but Koine Greek, the first-century equivalent of colloquial English. I wouldn't have shouted at the money changers in the temple courts—can't go alienating important market segments, you know.

And, no doubt, the world would still be lost.

If I were in charge, people would receive the desires of their hearts. In the last chapter, I mentioned a pain from my past—now I want to mention a pain from my present. I don't understand why God "allows" my husband and me to struggle so often with money. Sure, compared to much of the world, we're rolling in affluence, but most of us don't compare ourselves to, say, Stone Age peoples in New Guinea. We compare ourselves to others in our "tribe," peers in our church and community, people we grew up with, people we work with. This has been one of my major thorns over the years. I wonder, *God, what are you doing here?* We're not materialistic; if anything, we're frugal to a fault. If we had more money we wouldn't spend it foolishly. We'd send our daughter to a Christian school and support various deserving ministries and okay, *maybe* build an addition on our house. I get irritated at God because it seems so unfair that both my husband and I should be liberal-arts types; couldn't at least *one* of us have been born with computer skills, or perhaps an interest in health care? My brother-in-law just got an electrical engineering degree; he has his pick of lucrative job offers. I don't even know what an electrical engineer does.

Money struggles bring out the worst in me. I wrestle with envy, needless fretting, self-centeredness—all decidedly unbiblical, unspiritual behaviors. Worry over money causes me to focus *too much* on money (kind of like when you're dieting—all you think about is food), and not enough on "whatever is of good report."

It's sometimes tough for me to see how I'm being "refined" through all of this. But God knows. It could simply be—I'm guessing here—that God is preparing me so that when I have a huge bestseller, I'll remember the hard times and not get puffed up.

All right, just kidding. Actually, it could be that the process *itself*—my praying, my wondering, my attempts to apply Scripture to our situation—pleases God. There have been times, many times, when my trials have driven me to a radical dependence on him, that jumping-into-the-net feeling.

Is Anybody Else Up There?

Right now you may feel like you're clinging to a tenuous branch and have been there way too long. Isn't that one of the most painful feelings, that sense of interminable struggle and, especially, the uncertainty? Why doesn't anything come easy? Why is there not a resolution?

It can be a frightening place. You've heard the familiar story about the man who falls off the cliff. At the last minute he grabs a branch sticking out of the precipice and clings to it, yelling, "Help! Help! Is anybody up there? Help!"

"I will help you," booms a voice from on high. "If you let go of the branch, I will catch you."

There's a pause. Then: "Is anybody *else* up there?"

This story illustrates how we aren't usually grateful for those hard and risky experiences. But jumping off that cliff always turns out to be the very best thing for us, because of who we find waiting at the bottom to catch us—and who we become during that seeming free fall.

A certain woman, Ellen, as I'll call her, fits into this category. She has faced chronic money troubles, difficulties with a teenager, and her husband's employment ups and downs. When we see each other we laugh and commiserate and get down to nitty-gritty honesty. Sometime back, while still in the midst of a lot of unresolved stuff, she said to me, "I don't know what God is doing. But I've come to realize I have to trust him no matter what. I know he cares—to think otherwise implies that I think he doesn't love me. I feel a lot more at peace now."

Stretch Marks of Faith

Sometimes all we can do is take one baby step off that cliff. We may not be ready to jump wholeheartedly, but we can at least admit that God is up to something. We choose to trust him, and we're eager to discover what that "something" is. We are finally able to open the door—just a crack—and allow him to begin his work in us.

Not to open that door, to fight God and resist his goodness, to succumb to resentment and bitterness, is to miss out on experiences that could be the making of us—like choosing not to have a baby because we're afraid we'll get stretch marks.

I've watched Ellen accumulate a few spiritual "stretch marks" over the years. I've seen in her evidence that the hard thing is the best thing; evidence of a tested and *lived* faith, something deep and dimensional and textured. She's not yet forty and her face is smooth and fresh, but her faith reminds me of the face of an elderly person whose wrinkles proudly display a life fully lived—lines of sorrow and humor and weariness, lines born of squinting into the sun, and lines born of raising eyebrows in amazement.

When Anne Shirley of Green Gables prepares to wed Gilbert Blythe in the garden of the old homestead, she observes that a house becomes a home when it has witnessed a birth, a death, and a marriage. I wonder if, likewise, we can become more "at home" within ourselves as we experience similar joys and losses and risks in commitment.

It's important to tell one another stories of those times we felt as if we were tumbling down a cliff, only to land in a green valley next to a stream. I plan to keep talking about my childbirth experience, and I'm going to keep listening to and learning from people like Ellen.

God is always up to something, bringing the best out of the worst—even though it may not seem like it at the time. Can you trust him? Can you—with me—take that baby step off the cliff, open that door? Through that opening we might just hear God saying, to paraphrase Scripture, "Have you considered my servant, (your name here)? There is none like her!"

Chapter Three

Living Beyond Our Limits

What did women do for an excuse before PMS was invented?

This question occurred to me one recent Saturday. By all logic I should have felt great. My mother would soon arrive for a long-awaited visit, we had watched my daughter score in her basketball game, the weather was okay.

We were on our way home from the car wash (you know you need to get out more when your idea of "making memories" is a family outing to watch the undercarriage spray come on), and we passed the house of a girl Amanda knows—a girl who was having a birthday party to which my daughter had not been invited. In the driveway a group of girls were piling into a van. "There's Megan's party," Amanda said, with a scorn I imagined was an effort to hide her pain.

That did it. All the feelings of childhood rejection came flooding back, accompanied by tears. I went on about how we had invited Megan to our parties in the past and, hello-o, invitations are supposed to be reciprocal and Megan's one of those sickeningly perfect Christian kids and nobody knows how to be a true friend and what's wrong with this world anyway ... I mean, if I'd gone on much longer I would have started bawling about vanishing species of newts.

In other words, I was doing some serious overreacting.

By now Fritz and Amanda were giving me bemused, somewhat alarmed looks—*There's something wrong with Mom!* There was, but I felt as if I couldn't help myself. I could sense this *bzzz* vibrating through my nervous system, the way I sometimes feel after serious caffeine overload. Only I hadn't drunk that much coffee. My nerves felt like the sheathing was peeling off, exposing bare and vibrating wire.

There's only one thing to do when I feel like that. When we got home I said to Fritz, "I think I have PMS." He ran into the bathroom, grabbed two Midols and some water, and practically forced the pills down my throat. He did everything except spread peanut butter on them, the way one does when giving a dog his medicine. (There are times I don't even have to tell Fritz I have PMS. He simply looks at me falling apart, disappears, and returns a moment later with tranquilizers. Does Promise Keepers teach men how to cope with their wives' hormones? It would be a wonderful service.)

I have a sixty-year-old friend who told me that since she's gotten older her emotions have smoothed out. I can't wait. For me, PMS usually comes crashing in, as it did on that Saturday. If I'm alone, it usually takes the form of a grandiose conclusion that the bedrock truth of my life is that I am alone in a howling wasteland and that all hope is sham and denial.

I've even had PMS descend on me at church. One moment I'll be singing along, my daughter nudging me to not sing so loud because "Mom, it's *so embarrassing* and people will *hear* you"; the next I'll suddenly look around and think, *We have no real friends in this church.*

It makes me understand why, after some awful crime, neighbors of the alleged perpetrator so often shake their heads and say, "I can't understand this. He was always so friendly." So am I, until the hormones start erupting.

But I don't want to be at the mercy of my biology, or the weather, or anything else. I am not my estrogen or progesterone or whatever else is bubbling around in there. I may be subject to PMS, but I don't have to let it ruin my day—and that of others. I may be sensitive to the weather, but there will be hot days, gray days, and cold days nonetheless.

In fact, I can figure it out: Let's say that out of 365 days in the year, about two-thirds of the time, say 240 days, the weather in Northern Illinois is unsatisfactory. Some of those 240 days are bound to overlap with the six weeks out of the year my PMS is at its worst (it seems to alternate months), meaning there's the potential for truly down-the-toilet days. Then factor in those times when the bank informs us we're seriously overdrawn or when the car dies in its sleep or when my daughter and I have a huge fight. Not that these things have actually happened much, but you see where I'm going. I'm left with maybe one week when life seems worth living.

I don't want to live like that. God doesn't want me to live like that.

Don't Fence Me In

God wants to use our struggles to yield rich and lasting fruit in us. He can only do this if we resist the tendency to let ourselves be *defined* by our struggles—by our limitations. There's a significant difference between saying, "I suffer" and "I'm a sufferer," between saying, "I failed" and "I'm a fail-ure." We do not have to be controlled by PMS or bad days or lack of money or even physical handicaps. (I think one of the healthiest advances in language in the last few years is the use of the term "person with a disability," as opposed to "disabled person.") Nor are we trapped by our family legacies or by where we grew up or by our temperaments or a host of other things. Through Christ, God frees us to *transcend* our limitations, to somehow become bigger than those things that fence us in. Christ calls all of us to "rise and walk!"—with our eyes fixed on him.

Paul talks about this frequently in his letters: becoming a new creation, putting off the old nature, renewing our minds, not being conformed. I've always had trouble understanding his "content in all circumstances" statements in Philippians. In fact, I have thought, *Okay for you, Paul; you were the apostle to the Gentiles. But I can't even get my own kid to listen to me sometimes.* Still, his message is the same for all of us, no matter our circumstances. We may get shipwrecked or thrown into prison, where we crouch in a corner, shivering with leg irons cutting into our flesh. Our corporation may downsize us out of a job. We may be hurt by someone we care about. Perhaps we suffer from depression. Or maybe we're just kind of moody and pessimistic. As the old Four Tops song goes: " . . . can't help myself . . ."

But Jesus announced his fulfillment of Isaiah's scripture: "Here I am, ready to proclaim release to the captives!" (See Luke 4:18.) God came to earth not only to free us *from* something—our sins—but to lead us *toward* something— his Kingdom. Life to the fullest. Life beyond whatever our circumstances may be, on into eternity.

Overcome—or Transcend?

We do not necessarily overcome our circumstances. There's a big difference between transcending and overcoming. I think of Robertson McQuilkin, the former head of Columbia Bible College in South Carolina. For years he has cared for his wife, Muriel, who has Alzheimer's disease. He wrote eloquently in *Christianity Today* about his love for Muriel, his lifelong partner, and his joy in being able to minister to her even though, often, she doesn't even know who he is. Muriel will not be "cured" of her illness. She will not overcome her circumstances this side of heaven.

I suspect that for many married couples—or children of aging parents—Alzheimer's is like a lurking, "what-if?" shadow. Most of us shudder at the prospect of someone we love being taken over by this terrible affliction, which seems to steal the very humanity from its victims. I look at my strong and vital husband, at the way he can make me double over with laughter by acting silly, at the theological discussions we have, at the brisk walks we enjoy, and I cannot conceive of his becoming helpless and incontinent and calling me by the wrong name. But we are not immune: What if the worst were to happen, to me or to any of us, as it did to the McQuilkins?

We can't change our outward circumstances, but we do have a choice: We can sink into bitterness and despondency, or we can receive God's grace and pray that he may use us, even through the worst of times.

A Great Soul in a Tiny Frame

Jane Hess Merchant was another "transcender." You've probably never heard of her. I hadn't either, until I came across her biography, *A Window on Eternity*, several years ago. This amazing woman lived from 1920 to 1972. A Christian poet, she suffered from a rare condition called osteogenesis imperfecta, or "brittle-bone disease." If she so much as took a step, she risked breaking a bone. So she was forced to spend her life in bed. She lost her hearing, and then most of her sight in one eye. And Jane was no bigger than a child— only four feet tall.

Yet, her soul towered like the Tennessee mountains she loved.

Jane once quoted the famous preacher Harry Emerson Fosdick: "We all have cellars in our house, but we don't have to live in them." While she frequently battled depression and discouragement, she also published numerous books of poetry and devotions. She dug into Scripture and carried on lengthy correspondence with friends from all over the world. She loved watching God's creation through her window. Her work was compared to that of Emily Dickinson—another shut-in who, unlike Jane, chose her confinement. Jane, perhaps a more rebellious and vigorous spirit (that's one reason I like her so much; she kicked at what was and looked toward what could be), would never have shut herself in the house had she had a choice.

She didn't have a choice. But her soul ranged far and wide, always seeking God, growing an intense and absolutely life-giving relationship with him. She wrote to one of her friends: "With [Christ], everything has meaning and significance, even the things that seem completely cruel and senseless. And that, I know, is a rather repetitious conclusion, having been repeated by millions of people down through the years. And I know that to many, if not most, of the philosophers and wise men it seems a very simple-minded conclusion, besides. *But it isn't superficial with me.*"

Jane Merchant was "more than a conqueror." But she was no plaster saint. Sometimes we find it hard to identify with people who have transcended some grievous circumstance, because the things that cause us pain seem almost banal by comparison—like PMS. I cannot relate to Jane's physical circumstances, but I *can* connect with her shyness, her discouragement about her writing, the gloom that seized her from time to time. Across the decades she whispers to me that I, too, can transcend bad days and bounced checks, and that it's okay to sometimes feel rebellious and cantankerous. She teaches me, again, the truth of Paul's statement that God chose the weak things of this world to shame the strong. I wish I could have had her as a friend.

"Lying There, He Grew Bigger"

Franklin D. Roosevelt was, in a way, both weak and strong. It has always fascinated me how he was able to rise above his silver-spoon upbringing and forge a new pact between government and citizenry. Today we take it for granted that the poor, the elderly, and the infirm won't be left to starve in the streets. Even the most ardent anti-big-government conservatives agree that government has *some* role in caring for the needy. That wasn't always the case. There was a time when ragged, hungry orphans wandered the streets of New York City right outside iron gates behind whose protection railroad barons dined in splendor. FDR, the pampered only child of a family who traced its lineage back to the first Dutch and English settlers of the 1600s, could have stayed behind the gates. Instead, he grew into the visionary and compassionate leader who changed society forever.

It took polio to change Roosevelt. Before the disease struck him in 1921, he had been, according to those who knew him, a likable but somewhat arrogant young man. Then, in the painful months that followed, as he lay in bed working to recover movement in his limbs, he had a lot of time to think, to reflect. His son James said of this period, "Lying there, he grew bigger." He had suffered; now he could empathize with others who were hurting and help-less, those who couldn't pull themselves up by their boot-straps because they had no boots. He rose above both the narrowness of his sheltered childhood and his disability. As his legs withered from disuse, his spirit broadened and deepened.

One question keeps popping up throughout this book, perhaps because I keep wondering about it but also because there are different ways we can look at it: Couldn't FDR have learned empathy through, for instance, visiting settle-ment houses in poor areas of Manhattan? (He did, actually; Eleanor volunteered at one and he was shaken by what he saw.) Did Paul have to ask God three times to remove his thorn? Couldn't Job have gotten the message after one cat-astrophe? Doesn't God make it kind of rough on us?

Only, perhaps, because he wants to really stre-e-etch us. There's that sense that we've talked about, that God wants to upend our expectations, to surprise us with his power, to challenge us: *Brace yourself! Look! Look at me and won-der at my glory!* He will do anything to bring us to obedi-ence—into a relationship with him.

Gnawing Through the Ropes

To watch God at work is to receive a revelation of just how powerful he is—unloosening our shackles the way the mice in *The Lion, the Witch, and the Wardrobe* gnawed through the ropes that bound Aslan. I've seen him work in my own life time and again, and he has had to do some pretty intri-cate untying to get me out of certain self-imposed traps. No, I'm not crippled or coping with a dread disease, but my traps are legion; one self-imposed snare has been my reliance on outward signs of success to confirm my worth as a person. It's all tangled up with those negative adolescent experiences, a fear of rejection, and a longing to be affirmed and recognized. I'm good because I have friends, because I have a great family, because I have a nice house and a career. For years I believed this, and I was happy as long as everything was "going well." But when it wasn't . . .

I can resonate with something Philip Yancey, who probably suffers from the same melancholic, introspecting-too-much burden as I do, says. He writes of sitting at O'Hare Airport for five hours, waiting for a flight, feeling "burdened by other people's pains and sorrows, doubts and unanswered prayers." Author Karen Mains happened to be waiting for the same flight, and they talked—or, rather, Philip talked and Karen listened. "Then out of nowhere she asked a question that has always stayed with me," says Philip. "'Philip, do you ever just let God love you?' she said. 'It's pretty important, I think.'"

At this very late stage, I'm discovering what that means—to just let God love me. Not for what I do, but because it's who God, incarnate in Christ, is, and because somewhere along the way he chose me to be his child. My response has been a bit like Sally Field's when she won the Oscar a number of years back: "You like me! You really like me!" It's delightful and surprising and very, very freeing. I'm able to just . . . *be*, and know it's okay.

The Endless Horizon

Suffering has been my teacher, the self-imposed suffering of years of recurrent discouragement and the feeling that, no matter what happened, there was a needy, empty core at my center. I don't think I decided to "choose joy," as some people advocate, because I don't believe it's that simple and I don't have that kind of upbeat temperament. I have, however, felt God's grace working its way into those little broken cracks. The joy is that he chooses us—and in so doing, frees us to let ourselves be loved and to go beyond our limits.

The ultimate lesson of living beyond those limits is, finally, that this life with its traps and fences is not all there is. When we keep our eyes fixed on Jesus, he beckons us to follow him to that endless horizon, where we will "rise and walk" with him—forever.

Chapter Four

I Cried Till I Laughed

I think my husband may need to stop taking me to the movies. I'm such an embarrassing date.

Unless the film is outright, hilarious slapstick, I always manage to find something to cry about. We just saw *Babe* over the weekend. Based on the ads, I wasn't sure I'd like it. Well, I *loved* it. It was imaginative and thought-provoking and had real emotional weight. And, of course, it made me cry. I cried when Fly, the mother sheep dog, was talking about Rex, the proud father sheep dog, and his heroic past; the camera showed Rex in the present, lying forlorn and muzzled, following surgery to take away his aggressiveness. (Count on me crying when the story involves a dog. Ann Landers periodically runs this really sentimental bit of verse. It's called something like "A Dog's Prayer"—maybe you've seen it—and toward the end it says something like, "And when my step grows slow and my eyes grow dim . . ." at which point I always start bawling.) I choked up when the normally taciturn Farmer Hoggett sang and danced to revive the sick Babe. I misted over at the end when he said to Babe, "That'll do, pig."

I cried at *Apollo 13* when the spacecraft roared off the launch pad; it was such a symbol of man's soaring aspiration.

And then there's *Little Women*. When Beth died, I just sobbed. And let's not even talk about *E.T.* Fortunately, everyone else in the theater is often sniffling and honking too. It feels oddly heartening. We've all heard about the disappearance of "community" in America, but it's an interesting exercise in communal bonding to sit in a darkened room with a hundred or so other strangers, all of whom are gulping and blowing their noses. It makes you feel like it's not such a bad old world after all.

A Public Spectacle

Of course, inside the theater nobody can really *see* you. Columnist Bob Greene shares some thoughts about public emotion after he witnessed a particular scene in a New York airport. A woman was engaging in behavior so unusual, so far from what is acceptable public demeanor, that passersby reacted with confusion, not knowing whether to avert their eyes or stare in shock.

Was the woman indecently clad? Babbling to herself? Being drunk and disorderly? Actually, if you live in or have spent any time in New York, these behaviors may not even seem so out of the ordinary. You just look right through the strangeness with that unseeing city stare and go on your way.

No, this woman was doing none of the above. What she *was* doing was crying. "One minute," writes Greene, "she was walking down the airport concourse, a traveler among hundreds. The next moment she was sobbing. . . . wrenching, shaking tears." Just an ordinary woman, about twenty-eight years old, dressed in business clothes, striding on her way, part of the stream of humanity flowing through the airport—sobbing, louder and louder.

Greene muses on this: "The surprising thing is not that this woman was sobbing in the airport. The surprising thing—maybe—is that it doesn't happen more often. The surprising thing is that such a scene catches people by surprise. All the people behind those masks of bland contentment—are they, in truth, closer to the placid emotions symbolized by those masks, or are they sometimes secretly a little closer to the woman sobbing in the midst of them?"

When I was a kid, I used to imagine what would happen if people radically departed from normal public behavior—for example, if a man mailing something at the post office looked at the clerk behind the counter and snapped, "Your glasses are ugly!" Instead, we have learned civil and appropriate behavior. We don't bawl in public—usually. But Greene is right. We are all sometimes "secretly a little closer" to that sobbing woman. Crying in the movies hurts so good. Crying—or simply feeling pain—because we're suffering just plain *hurts*.

But here again, God can turn what looks like a bad thing into something beautiful and redemptive.

How Are You, Really?

Part of the problem with suffering and struggling is that we can just feel so *lousy*. We wonder what is wrong with us if we don't "get better." I recently read something on "tips for workplace behavior." One of the tips: When someone asks you how you are, *never* say anything except "Fine." Weeping and confessing to emotional weakness are frowned upon in our culture. We admire the stoicism of a Rose Kennedy, gazing impassively from under a black veil as her son's flag-draped casket rolls by to the muffled cadence of a drum. (Thirty-plus years later, I can still recall that sound. I don't remember anything about the algebra I was trying to learn at the time, but I remember that mourning drum.) Even in the church, we prefer victory speeches to admissions of struggle. It's okay to *have struggled*, past tense, and then share a wonderfully uplifting testimony of how we conquered that weakness; it isn't as okay to still be in the midst of the pain. People get tired of hearing about it. They don't want to know how we are, really.

And yet . . .

Last Sunday was Palm Sunday. For our adult-education hour, I put together a special presentation on Jesus: Who is this we shout "Hosanna!" to? Through Scripture readings and personal reflections, a portrait emerged of a Man who loves us unconditionally. His ways of connecting with us are infinitely creative and wholly personalized. Jesus the challenger: "Seize the day!" Jesus the provider: "Ask and you shall receive." Jesus the miracle worker: "Lazarus, come forth!" Jesus the grieving friend, the One who understands our suffering—because he's been there.

In worship we sang "Man of Sorrows, What a Name." Oh, how I love that hymn. You want to talk about weeping. . . . The tears just flowed, I was so overwhelmed with Christ's humanity and divinity and so overcome with love for him.

Turn Not from His Grief Away

One way we can move closer to Jesus, one unexpected gift of sorrow, is that we can *identify* with him in his suffering. Not just to think in terms of "what he did for us," but to "watch with him one bitter hour," as the words of another of my favorite hymns says it.

We too often think of Christ's suffering as something glorious and almost abstract. We use words like "atonement," which are fine theologically but which can distance us from the physical reality of spike-like nails being driven into tender flesh. We proclaim, with Isaiah, that "by his stripes we are healed," but it was not *we* who bowed under the Roman lash, with its weighted tips, as the guards looked on and jeered.

Hebrews tells us that "Since the children have flesh and blood, [Christ] too shared in their humanity so that by his death he might destroy him who holds the power of death.... For this reason he had to be made like his brothers in every way, in order that he might become a merciful and faithful high priest in service to God, and that he might make atonement for the sins of the people. Because he himself suffered when he was tempted, he is able to help those who are being tempted" (2:14, 17–18).

"Made like his brothers in every way." An insight from one of our Palm Sunday speakers helped me understand what this really means. He speculated on what it must have been like for Jesus to be, in effect, the God-boy. "How did the boy Jesus deal with the town bully?" he wondered. "How did he relate to his brothers and sisters? Did Joseph ever say, 'Jesus, where's my hammer? I know you took it!'" He talked about the pain and humiliation that childhood brings, of Jesus being, as far as we know, homeless at the age of thirty. Was he ever lonely?

Scripture does show Jesus weary, hungry, thirsty. It does show him rejected by the men in the Nazareth synagogue. That must have hurt—like returning to your home church as a guest speaker and having everyone laugh at you. And how did he feel when Peter, his chief lieutenant, turned away from him and ran off into the darkness like a furtive coyote? Yes, he *knew* all this would take place. But he "shared in [our] humanity." And so, *knowing* made it no easier. As my pastor once observed, "Jesus cried out to God on the cross. But who among us would say, 'No, Jesus, you shouldn't feel that way. You of all people know how it comes out!'"

"Good to See You"

Jesus was not ashamed to cry out. Neither should we be. To freely weep means to understand a bit of what our Lord went through. And to understand what our Lord went through opens us up to receive his compassion and cling to his faithfulness. We know that, as much as he sorrowed and suffered, he is also Lord. He can, in David Mains's vivid analogy, "talk us through" our struggles the way Gary Sinise, who played the grounded astronaut in *Apollo 13*, talked Kevin Bacon through the power-up procedures needed to revive the lifeless command module and get the crew back home.

There's another time during this movie that I cried . . . when, after the tense silence of the blackout period during reentry, the chutes open up and Tom Hanks says, "Good to see you," and the music swells. I cried even though I knew how it would come out.

I saw the real Marilyn Lovell, wife of astronaut Jim Lovell, recently on a PBS documentary about the mission. She says she still gets choked up, more than a quarter-century later, thinking about what could have happened to her husband. Because, even with all the technical expertise and can-do ingenuity at their disposal, neither the astronauts nor the Mission Control personnel really did know how the story would end. There was a very real possibility the men could have been lost.

In much the same way, we don't know exactly how our particular story will come out in the end. But as we cling to Christ, to his faithfulness and to his guidance, we know that we *will* come out.

Blinded by The Night-Light

How bright the sunshine is after blundering around in the dark. When I was in sixth grade, I spent the night at a friend's house. This was my first sleepover there, as I didn't like my friend's parents much. Her mother yelled at us if we ventured into the white-carpeted living room, and her father was a kind of tough guy who came home from work and sat around at the kitchen table in his undershirt. (My mom never yelled, and my dad didn't go around in Fruit of the Loom.) Anyway—wouldn't you know it—in the middle of the night I had to get up and go to the bathroom. My friend's bedroom was completely dark, almost black—not even an illuminated clock dial or a glow from a street light. Sleepy, I became disoriented. I couldn't remember where the bedroom door was. Panic seized me as I groped for the knob and felt around with my hands for a window or some piece of furniture that might offer a clue as to where I was. Meanwhile, I tried desperately not to crash about and wake the entire household. I didn't want the undershirted father coming in and yelling at me.

It was a thoroughly horrible feeling, almost vertiginous, and it seemed to go on for hours, though it was probably only a few minutes. Finally I found the door, opened it—and behold, there was light! A pale, greenish glow emanated from the night-light in the bathroom down the hall. I've never felt so grateful for such weak light in my life. My world was right again. Things were in balance.

If we never experience the darkness, what meaning does the light hold? If we never go all the way down, how can we test our foundations? If we never have the experience of unabashed lament, like Jeremiah, how can we truly live the prophet's affirmation that God's mercies are "new every morning" (Lam. 3:23)? How can we truly understand the mighty promise of Revelation, that he "will wipe every tear" from our eyes?

Doffing the Armor

To sorrow without shame removes the armor of our prideful self-sufficiency and opens us up to healing. Recently my daughter and I took the train downtown to the Art Institute in Chicago. This world-class museum holds treasures of French Impressionist art, classics such as Grant Wood's *American Gothic*, an extensive collection from Picasso's Cubist period . . . but somehow I always seem to wind up in the armor exhibit. Probably because it's on the way to the restaurant. Amanda and I had read C. S. Lewis's *The Last Battle* a few months before, and in the story the last king of Narnia gives Jill and Eustace suits of mail to wear. I had never known exactly what "mail" was until I saw it at the Art Institute. It's not the same as armor. A mail shirt is made out of hundreds of little iron rings. From a distance it looks like some kind of glittery material, like the medieval equivalent of one of those beaded tops fashionable women wear to Christmas parties. But don't try to penetrate it!

Keeping a stiff upper lip is something like donning a mail of the soul. Weeping implies a loss of control, as if we haven't mastered our emotions. Isn't that a telling figure of speech? If we master our emotions too completely, are we leaving enough room for the *Master*?

It's natural to want to have some sense of control, of course. One of my struggling friends—a member of my visible cloud of witnesses who have surrounded and inspired this book—is dealing with a lot of unresolved stuff. She has that hanging-on-tenterhooks sense that can be so unpleasant. She told me the other day that her present challenge is especially painful because "it strikes at the core of how I relate to God—my need for certainty and control."

Doffing our mail and yielding control to God is an ongoing process. It's somewhat oxymoronic to imagine that we can simply make a decision to not be controlling. Think about that for a minute. We cannot make a decision to not control any more than we can decide to fill ourselves with God's grace.

The Embrace of the Father

But we can begin with our humanity—our "vulnerability," as Anne Lindbergh put it. We *do* lose control when we weep, when we freely acknowledge our sorrow. And that's all right. It's another of the unexpected gifts of suffering. Honest tears are part of the rain that softens our soil and makes us more porous, more open to the things of God. It's another way we become *real*.

Now, I'm not saying everyone has to be like me, choking up at doggerel verse or even crying easily and often. But think of how it is with a child who storms and weeps and struggles. As a parent, you hold her and comfort her. Eventually the crying subsides into an occasional sniffle, and she becomes quiet. If she is very small, she may fall asleep, and then you carry her off to her bed for a needed rest. If she's older, you may say gently, "All right. Now, can we talk about it?"

It's the same way with the Father and we who are his children. I know that some Christians today are troubled by "masculine" images of God, and I understand their concerns. But for me, limited by what I know, the picture of an all-wise, all-loving, all-just, and all-powerful heavenly Father gives me a way to connect with the Almighty. And, especially in times of suffering, this picture is more comforting, more of a very present help in time of trouble, than some abstract "force."

This Father invites us to come to him fragile, needy, trusting. Not armored in self-sufficiency, but open to his grace. It gets back to Paul's idea of strength perfected in weakness—and to Christ's reminder that we are, indeed, blessed when we mourn, for we shall be comforted. Comforted by him, the Man of Sorrows, who has borne our grief all the way to the Cross and who points to the light after the darkness—the glow shining from the empty tomb. Hallelujah! What a Savior!

Chapter Five

Hey, Did You Hear the One About the Leaky Roof?

Too many years ago, around the time the Beatles first became popular, some folksy-type group released a hit song that included a chorus about not letting the rain come down because the roof had a hole in it and they might drown. Cute little lyrics. Cute until it happens to you.

It happened thusly: Last fall I was sitting at my desk doing what I always do, which is work. It was a dark, dreary, damp, depressing day—all those downer "d" words. Raining. I got up and went into another room for some reason, and all of a sudden I heard this strange sound.

Ploink. Ploink.

Well, perhaps one of the gutters was leaking a bit, or it was the rain dripping onto the place where the stovepipe vents to the outside. Nothing to wor—

Ploink.

Oh, dear. This did not sound good. This sounded like *indoors.* I peered out onto the porch/workspace, where, what to my wondering eyes should appear but a very long drop in the shape of a tear. It was coming from the ceiling. I could see the little hole.

Well, if *that* doesn't endanger your sense of earthly security, to have the very roof over your head open up to the heavens. I started muttering to myself, as I always do when I'm really ticked off at inanimate objects or events out of my control: "I can't believe this. Of all times. Like I really need this. Life stinks." Then I went to get some buckets and spent the rest of the day bailing and feeling sorry for myself.

Besides, it was just so dark outdoors. Not in a nice, cozy way where you can make yourself a cup of tea and curl up with a good book. No, it was kind of scary dark, with sheets of torrential rain and occasional lightning. I love lightning when it comes at the end of a sultry summer day, but in November it seems, I don't know, *wrong*.

The next day, however, I awoke to something very right—that soft white glow that signals the first winter snow. Oh, did *that* ever feel nice. I snuggled down into the flannel sheets next to my husband, secure in the knowledge that the leak had frozen. I felt great all day—exhilarated, almost Christmasy. And I was able to get my sense of humor back.

I've already talked about how much brighter the light can seem after a time of stumbling through the dark, how hard times cause me to appreciate life's small blessings all that much more. Just as suffering teaches us the healing value of honest lament, it also leads us to look for joy and laughter, to experience a deepened sense of gratitude for . . . well, just life.

The Gift of Sitting Around at Home

This came home to me powerfully as I watched the 1996 Academy Awards. You might remember the Holocaust survivor who urged those of us sitting at home to treasure our freedom, the gift of "an ordinary evening at home"—something denied the men and women and children who huddled behind the walls of Auschwitz and Dachau and Bergen-Belsen.

My daughter read Anne Frank's diary a while back. I hadn't read it for years, so I returned to the book with great interest. One of the most poignant aspects of this remarkable document is the contrast between Anne's "normal" life and her existence in the Secret Annex. At first, she spoke blithely about school, boyfriends, movies, arguments with her mother—all the everyday stuff of a thirteen-year-old's life. She complained about the hot weather. Then, after the Franks went into hiding, such rare treats as a cake became an occasion for celebration. A breath of fresh air through the attic window was something to inhale deeply.

The apostle Paul, of course, knew about looking for rays of hope in the darkness of prison. His words of encouragement must have been a lifeline to the young churches, both during and after his lifetime. Paul himself lived long enough to see the crazed Nero ascend to the imperial throne and launch a mass persecution of Christians. I've heard it suggested that Nero personally ordered Paul's execution. Clearly, this itinerant and aging Jew was a threat to the peace of the Empire! Yet the fire of the Spirit would not be quenched. The church continued to grow, fed by words like these: "It is strength that endures the unendurable and spills over into joy, thanking the Father who makes us strong enough to take part in everything bright and beautiful that he has for us" (Col. 1, THE MESSAGE).

The Wheelchair on the Interstate

Last night Amanda and I were watching a Bull's playoff game when NBC went dark. We started channel surfing and a man being interviewed on the local Christian TV station caught Amanda's eye—an oddly disfigured man. "Mom, look at this guy," she said. At first I was startled, even repulsed. Then I cried, "Wait a minute! That's Dave Roever!"

Dave Roever was severely injured in Vietnam. His face was practically blown apart and he's undergone many reconstructive surgeries. Now he has an evangelistic ministry; he speaks to large audiences, talking openly about his scars, how God has used them, and how God can heal anything. Roever himself makes as much of an impact as his message. His eyes twinkle, and his mouth, slightly twisted, smiles a lot. Host Jerry Rose asked him if he ever questioned God about why this had happened. Roever grinned. "No, I think I'm afraid to ask," he said. "I'm afraid God might say, 'Well, Roever, there's just something about you I don't like!'"

I loved that. I loved that he didn't just answer with some pious cliché. I loved his obvious relish for life—his "enduring the unendurable." On a day when Michael and Scottie and the rest of the Bulls were gearing up for another basketball championship, I thought, *Here is a hero indeed.*

Humor under adversity—humor *about* adversity—is a special sort of grace that turns suffering on its ear. We are moved by the courage of Christopher Reeve following his paralysis from a riding accident. He appeared on the same Academy Awards program as the Holocaust survivor. Following a standing ovation, he quietly said, "What you may not know is that I left New York in September to get here in time." (The Oscar presentations are held in March.)

Talk about upending our expectations! Too often, we tend to treat those who are disabled with a sort of reverent pity. We may expect them to be wiser or more forbearing, but we do not expect them to be funny, certainly not at their own expense. Thinking of Reeve, I was convulsed by the image of a guy in a wheelchair, scooting west along the interstate. What both Reeve's and Roever's humor said to me was: "Ha ha! Fooled you! You thought I'd be long-faced at worst, martyrlike at best. Well, I'm bigger and braver than this affliction, and I want you to laugh along with me."

"How Can You Laugh When Dad Is Dying?"

Most of us will never know what it's like to face a gas chamber, paralysis, lions in an arena, or any one of many other traumatizing events that may be part of the challenge for us. When you're *really* in pain, looking for joy takes on a life-giving urgency: you laugh or go crazy. You either beat the affliction or end up confined to a home somewhere.

When the hurt is strong but not really unendurable, it can be even trickier sometimes. You might, for example, be out playing with your children on a beautiful day, when the thought occurs to you: *I have no money*. You can become consumed with worries about work or your teenagers or that funny recurring pain in your arm, and it eats away at you and steals your joy.

When my father was sick and in the hospital, everything seemed somehow dimmed by the shadow of his sorrowful passage. I would see some happy group laughing on the street or in a restaurant and fume, *How can you possibly be laughing when my father is dying?* I could hardly sit down to watch some mindless TV show—and therefore escape—because every time the phone rang I would jump, fearing the worst. Operation Desert Storm was brewing around this time, but I didn't pay much attention. I was in the midst of my own tempest.

Thank God, Dad's suffering didn't last long. I believe it was a divine mercy that my father did not have to endure existence as a helpless, wheelchair-bound stroke victim.

Many people fight back from such indignities, but my father, who pitched in Class A baseball, was not one of them; he valued youth and vigor and independence. He would not have made a saintly patient. And so, early one March morning, he left us. I miss him terribly, but I know where he is (and have had some profoundly reassuring dreams that seem to back up my faith). The worst, really, was *before*. I wish now I had been more intentional about taking part in everything bright and beautiful, even in the midst of the darkness. It would not have dishonored my father for me to have laughed a bit more. He was probably the funniest man I ever knew.

The Best of Times, the Worst of Times

Paul reminds the Thessalonians that "although great trouble accompanied the Word, you were able to take great joy from the Holy Spirit!—taking the trouble with the joy, the joy with the trouble" (1 Thess. 1 THE MESSAGE). Think about it: life *usually* is a patchwork of joy and trouble, all happening at the same time. The roof leaks, then the first snow falls. Your favorite team is in the playoffs, but your TV is broken. If we wait until our troubles are over before looking for joy—kind of like how we avoid buying new clothes until we lose weight—we could be waiting a very long time, and missing what God has to offer.

One thing I loved about *Mr. Holland's Opus*, the wonderful film starring Richard Dreyfuss as a high school music teacher, was its scope, the way it showed the breadth and depth and complexity of an entire life; the ups, the downs, the joy, the trouble. In one scene, you see a prancing, uni-formed Mr. Holland leading the school marching band in the town's Fourth of July parade. His wife, beautifully played by Glenne Headly, and baby son are there on the sidelines, waving. Then the fire engines roll by, blaring their sirens. Babies cry and children plug their ears against the din. But as Mrs. Holland turns to her son, she sees that he is sitting placidly in his stroller, seemingly unaware of the noise.

It turns out that the boy is severely hearing impaired. Much of the movie turns on the tension between Mr. Holland's zest for introducing other people's children to the wonder of sound and his inability to communicate with his own son. Joy at work, trouble at home. It occurred to me that Holland's sorrow over his son actually intensified his passion for his work—his desire to focus on those areas of his life that *were* joyful. In time, he learns . . . but I won't spoil it for you by giving away the ending.

Any Excuse for a Party

If we look, we can always find reasons for joy. I'm afraid I misspent my youth glued to AM radio, which in those days wasn't news/talk, but played all the hits, all the time. (Reason to feel old number 837: recently Amanda's teacher asked her fifth-grade class, "How many of you know what a record player is?" About half had no clue.) One newscaster always ended his reports with a cheery, "Something to celebrate? Sure, there is!" He would then go on to talk about National Clean Out Your Refrigerator Week or some guy who had trained his dog to howl "Take Me Out to the Ball Game" or some such uplifting news.

Paul, in a sense, is saying something similar to the churches: *Something to celebrate? Sure, there is! You're growing in Christ. You have the hope of eternal life. Your fellowship is strong. You're pleasing to God.*

And God doesn't just leave his joy as an on-paper, abstract concept. He sends us specific events and people and delights—including those seemingly mundane evenings at home—to help us get through the hard times or, really, *any* time.

David Mains, in his recent book *When Life Becomes a Maze*, calls this process of celebration looking for "the joys that refresh our spirit." For Mains, as for the persecuted early church, this search has been an absolute necessity for spiritual survival. He writes honestly of his struggles. To condense a long and tangled story, Mains's Chapel Ministries went through huge financial losses and an uncertain future after a decades-long ministry devoted to strengthening the church. A major grant from a foundation fell through when the foundation collapsed. To keep his organization afloat, Mains had to take out a second mortgage on his house—at a time in life when most people are finally free and clear of such a burden. To top it all off, he and his wife, Karen, became the target of attacks from fellow Christians. Writing amid the crisis, Mains admits that many of the principles he affirms in his book are more by faith than by sight. Still, he writes, "I'm determined to keep track of the good. Lord knows I need it!"

Mains lists such "goods" as a family Christmas dinner, an open house with friends, even the donation of suits from a local clothier for him to wear on his TV show. We could, if we stopped and thought about it, come up with similar lists. But better than a list, perhaps, is to simply stand still and savor a moment while it's happening, even in the midst of trial. The point is to be intentional, particularly if one is temperamentally inclined toward brooding and analyzing things to death. It can feel almost defiant, like shaking a fist in Satan's face: "You're *not* going to discourage me, you liar."

Dishwashers or Clam Shacks?

Sometimes, when I'm doing something simple like walking my daughter to school on a bright spring morning, the robins singing and the lawnmowers sputtering to life, I'll think, *This really is the best God has for me.* I'm poignantly aware that these kinds of days are slipping by fast—you don't walk a junior high-aged kid to school.

I feel this way sometimes in church or sitting around my mother's kitchen table on Cape Cod or smelling the fragrance of new-mown hay out in farm country. It's all so sweet and precious, made more sweet by my memories of loneliness and spiritual wandering, more precious if I'm fully affirming the moment and not marring it with some needless anxiety like, *But I don't have another book contract.*

A related gift, perhaps, is the ability to sort out priorities and focus on what really matters—whatever is of "good report." I complain about money a lot, but, as I've said to my husband, "If God had to pick people to be broke, he probably did right in choosing us." We're not the type who enjoy recreational shopping. I'd rather go on a berry-picking outing with friends than schlep through one of those huge mall outlets (you always spend more money when you think you're getting bargains). We don't want the bother of a big house or the worry over someone stealing our worldly goods or the obsession over what the latest stock market dive means to our portfolio. We splurge on things like flowers and vegetables for the garden, and we have a wonderful time planting them.

It's not like we never spend, but we have been forced to make some choices, to think through what's really important to us: Do we buy a new dishwasher or take a Cape Cod vacation? I'd rather live with a few leaks and be able to stand at one particular spot on Nauset Beach on the Cape where I can see the ocean and hear the cries of blackheaded gulls and smell the odors from Liam's Clam Shack.

Jesus Laughed

Oh, by the way, the porch roof got fixed. Now Tom the Handyman says our entire roof needs replacing, to the tune of.... Oh, well, I won't think about that today. I just saw a rabbit hopping through the backyard. Someone's mowing their grass and it smells like clover. Amanda's out of school and maybe we can do something fun today. Father's Day is approaching and I can't wait to see the look on Fritz's face when he sees we got him ... a wrench. Okay, *and* a new set of sheets for our bed.

There's a lot that's wrong, but there's more that's right. As I go through this day, I'm sure I'll find something to laugh about. Maybe the joke will even be on me. There's no verse in Scripture that says, "Jesus laughed," but I'm certain he must have looked up at silly Zacchaeus in the sycamore tree and grinned in amusement. He must sometimes look down at silly *us* and chuckle. And I suspect it pleases him when we get the joke and laugh along with him.

Chapter Six

Walking by Faith . . . Toward What?

A while back Fritz and I were sitting on our front porch on one of the first really good evenings of spring we've had this year—"good" meaning you can be out-of-doors and not get drowned with rain or pelted with sleet. We like to do this, relax on our plaid sofa on the front porch. Nobody else in our neighborhood sits on *their* front porch, and certainly nobody else has dragged out an old plaid couch, but that's all right; we're sort of old and plaid ourselves. Even as I write this, I'm wearing my dad's forty-year-old checked Pendleton shirt. It's warm and comfortable and makes me feel good—and besides, how many people get to wear articles of clothing that are nearly as old as they are?

So we were lolling on the sofa, and as always happens in the spring, I got into a taking-stock mode; I looked around and thought about everything I would like to accomplish around the house and yard. Our property is a sort of work-in-progress. (Meaning, by the time we make any progress, we won't be working anymore.) We've gotten *some* things done—taken out some old bushes, painted the trim, planted a vegetable garden—but there's so much more. There always is, in an old house. We've lived here eight years, and everything seems to take *forever*. We accomplish things here and there, when we have money or time or when Tom the Handyman is available. So the basement goes unfinished and the old tree goes unfelled and the bathtub has these streaks we don't know how to get rid of, and by the time we're able to build a second story, we'll be unable to climb stairs.

I want my house to become what I, by faith, envisioned when we first moved in. I want to be like those people who moved into my childhood home and immediately built a huge new kitchen and family room. I get tired of waiting. I want some things *resolved*.

But I Don't *Want* to Play the Tortoise

Then there's my work. When things weren't going so well several years ago, I turned everything over to God (this is the Cliff's Notes version of a very long saga; you can find the unexpurgated version in my book *God, I Know You're Here Somewhere*), and the clear message I received was, *Hang in—Be faithful, as I am faithful.* In other words—you're fine, just keep on more or less doing what you're doing.

Thanks, Lord. I needed that. What I wanted to hear was some ringing, Jeremiah 29:11-like affirmation (funny how nobody ever quotes the passages where poor Jeremiah gets stuck in the cistern), but everything seemed to point to this unglamorous, unresolved, muddling-along sort of perseverance. Trudge along. Wait it out. Have faith.

I wanted to be a hare, but God was calling me to be a tortoise.

I remember the first time I heard that fable. I think I saw a cartoon version on TV, maybe on *The Mickey Mouse Club*. The story perplexed and even annoyed me: the cute little bunny should have beaten the ugly, plodding turtle! Of course I didn't quite get the message then; at six, one doesn't have to worry much about persistence.

Now, of course, I realize that speed will only get you so far. A tough shell is at least as much of an advantage.

Someday You'll Get This

I think it's significant that Anne Morrow Lindbergh mentions "patience" as one of the gifts of struggle. It may be *the* most important gift, because all the others—joy, vulnerability, compassion, openness, rising above our limitations, and the rest—can be hard to see when we're right in the midst of tough times. *God* can be hard to see. First, we have to do the faith-walk.

When Amanda was in kindergarten her teacher read the class a book titled *We're Going on a Bear Hunt*, a cute rhyming story about a family looking for a bear. The family keeps running into barriers, and every time they do, they repeat this verse: "We can't go around it. We can't go under it. We've got to go *through* it!"

If patience is the most important gift, it's also the most difficult for many of us to embrace. Even Jesus had his moment of wanting to avoid going *through* the trial he knew awaited him. As for the rest of us, we'd much prefer "suffering lite"—okay, I can stand anything for a couple of months or so. But *years?*

And yet I remember lessons learned at my mother's knee. When I was a kid I always got the sense from my mother, who understood Aesop's fable, that waiting for things was somehow character-building. I should feel sorry for those poor kids who always got whatever they wanted right away, because they'd grow into emotionally stunted adults who pursued their own shallow ends, such as petty

thievery and serial monogamy. She was always warning of
the dire consequences of something she called "instant
gratification." To her credit, she didn't say, "You'll thank me
someday," but I *am* grateful. I didn't get it then. I do now.

The Bible clearly says that perseverance builds character. It pleases God when we trust him through the darkness.
Many of the towering personages in Scripture found themselves in situations that went on and on and on: Noah on
the ark, Moses in the wilderness, Jeremiah living through
the Babylonian captivity.

We know all this intellectually, but we seldom celebrate
the process. We may even question it.

Are We There Yet?

You see, there's always the *then what?* question. We're
walking by faith, but aren't we getting somewhere? Won't
we eventually "sight" something? Walking by faith and not
by sight can sometimes seem like one of God's require-
ments that appear to go against human nature, especially in
our results-oriented culture. I can put up with almost anything if only I can see an end to it—if I know, for instance
that, while we may be strapped for money right now, in a
few weeks our income tax refund will arrive (unless I made
some egregious error). As hard as it was to lose my dad,
time has transformed the wound into a crooked, but bear-
able, scar.

What I have a problem with are those chronically unresolved situations. For example, I know a man who cannot
find a position in his chosen field—and he's looked for
years and years. How can he remain faithful without at
least some gleam of hope he's on the right track? What
does perseverance mean to the parents of a child whose disabilities are so profound that she requires institutionaliza-

tion, possibly in a less-than-ideal setting? Or how about the couple who are committed to staying together, even though they're emotional strangers to one another? God, this isn't *right!*

Where's the Victory?

It doesn't help when we read those "walking-by-faith" stories that always conclude with a successful outcome. Recently I read about a well-known author who, frustrated by attempts to get her first book published, "put the project in God's hands." The result was a several-million-copy best-seller. I don't mean to sound envious; I've read the book, and I believe God used it to touch many lives, including mine at an early stage of my Christian journey. It's just that such testimonies can make the rest of us feel like spiritual weaklings. Our "walk of faith" is often more like a limp. We, too, put some situation or person in God's hands, but healing doesn't happen or the crisis remains unresolved or the dream goes unfulfilled. Does this mean we didn't try hard enough, believe intensely enough, pray confidently enough?

We all know those who have been hurt by well-meaning believers who counseled during a time of need, "If you just had more faith. . . ." I used to think such attitudes were limited to the "name-it-and-claim it" school of Christianity, but they're not. The subtle danger of the "more faith" mentality is that it puts the emphasis on us—look what victorious Christians we are!—and not on God.

An Unsung Heroine

The Bible, as usual, tells a different story. When we think of examples of faith and perseverance in Scripture, we think of the "roll call of faith" in Hebrews, or maybe the persistent widow in Jesus' parable. But I'm more drawn to a woman nobody talks about much; she's sort of a sidebar to the main event. This nameless hemorrhaging woman appears in all three synoptic gospels, Matthew, Mark, and Luke, intercepting Jesus on his way to heal Jairus's daughter.

None of the Evangelists mention the exact nature of her bleeding, but it was probably some kind of a "female problem." Imagine having a twelve-year female problem! I can remember (if you'll permit me another childbirth reminiscence) how weak I felt from loss of blood after my daughter was born. The hospital put on a candlelight-and-steak dinner for new parents before they went home with their babies, and I remember I could hardly walk to the elevator and stand for the few minutes it took to get to the maternity ward. Then, a week later, I had to take Amanda back to the hospital for a blood test. After walking all over the place looking for the lab, I became dizzy and started to bleed heavily. I called my doctor's office and was told to go home, get off my feet, and stay there.

If such a relatively minor blood loss made me feel so weak, I can only guess how this woman felt, whether her condition was gynecological or something else. The Bible tells us, in one of those everyday kinds of details that give a texture of reality to an event, that "she had spent all she had on doctors." So not only was she sick, she had been impoverished by the health-care system, and I don't think the Romans had Medicaid. On top of that, Jewish law isolated menstruating women during their periods. Perhaps, then, she was shunned as unclean. The illness may have robbed her of her youth and looks.

Somehow, though, she had just enough hope, just enough strength left to touch Jesus' cloak. Notice that she didn't force herself upon the Master or badger him. Maybe she feared that Jesus, too, would reject her or lecture her if she accosted him face-to-face. Maybe she hoped she could slip away into the crowd unnoticed.

But this exhausted woman had just enough faith. That tentative plucking at Jesus' sleeve may have taken a leap of faith equivalent to, say, my deciding to live as a missionary among Amazon tribes without taking any food, money, or mosquito netting. In Eugene Peterson's paraphrase, Jesus responds by saying: "Courage, daughter. You took a risk of faith, and now you're well" (Matt. 9).

Reaching for Jesus' Cloak

Billy Graham tells the story of a woman named Linda whose immune system had been destroyed by chemicals. She was literally allergic to the world, something like the "boy in the bubble," and in and out of hospital isolation units for years. Graham quotes her: "I didn't think coherently. I was too busy trying to survive." She had only the energy to read one verse of Scripture a day and to pray for one minute. (This is actually more than many healthy people do. Talk about feeling convicted!)

Linda called even this small commitment "an overwhelming task." But it was enough. When her immunities were built up to the point where she could leave the isolation wards, she founded an organization called Direct Link, which connects people with disabilities to the help they need. "The Lord gave me suffering so I could help the suffering world of the disabled," she said.

There are times I identify with the nameless woman in the Gospels and with Linda more than I do with the bold adventurers of Scripture, the Sarahs and Esthers and even Mary herself. These two women are lionesses of faith, willing to believe and act on the impossible. I'm just me, more of a common tabby—not suffering a terrible ailment, but sometimes overwhelmed with ailments of the soul, often too weary and discouraged to pray anything more eloquent than, *Lord, be with me today.*

God Is Not a Drill Instructor

Yet it seems to be enough. Listen, again, to *The Message*:

The apostles came up and said to the Master, "Give us more faith." But the Master said, "You don't need *more* faith. There is no 'more' or 'less' in faith. If you have a bare kernel of faith, say the size of a poppy seed, you could say to this sycamore tree, 'Go jump in the lake,' and it would do it" (Luke 17).

Other passages echo a similar theme: the Kingdom as a pine tree seed, the miracle of the loaves and fishes, the idea that being faithful over a little means that one is faithful over much. Yet somewhere along the line we've gotten the idea that life in Christ is about tremendous exertions of belief, that God is like some Marine drill instructor who requires the impossible. But Christ knows our weaknesses; he understands our temptations (1 Cor. 10:13). He knows what it's like to be one of us—because he *was* one of us. He understands the challenge of walking by faith and not by sight, and, in his Holy Spirit, called the Comforter, he gives us Someone to walk with us. As we walk, that tiny seed of faith is nurtured and may well grow into a spreading tree, rooted in trust and reaching in hope.

When Life Sneaks Up on You

Perhaps, too, the walk *itself* is what matters—not the destination. You've heard the saying that goes something like, "Life is what happens to you while you're waiting for something else to come along." I mentioned the film *Mr.*

Holland's Opus earlier, how it shows that life mixes up the good and the bad, the joy and the sorrow. At the beginning of the movie Mr. Holland is just starting out his career as a music teacher. He sees this as a temporary occupation, a way to earn a living while he works toward his "real" vocation as a composer. He teaches during the day, then comes home and tinkers around on the piano at night, working on his symphony. Years pass, teaching absorbs more and more of his time and energy, and he hasn't gone to New York (unlike an ambitious student of his). In short, he isn't the new Leonard Bernstein. The film shows how Mr. Holland's "opus" is actually his life and what he has given to his students. While he was waiting, life sneaked up on him and said, "Surprise! This is good!"

Mr. Holland proved himself a faithful husband, father, teacher, even though he never reached the destination he was pursuing. But faithfulness though a dream is lost is one thing. What about faithfulness even though one has lost a child?

What Baby Richard Began

It is a story you may remember—one that, even now, brings tears to my eyes and fury to my soul. Kim and Jay Warburton, who live in suburban Chicago, were the adoptive parents of "Baby Richard," the boy whose biological father stepped forward to claim him. A bitter and much-publicized court battle ensued—a battle the Warburtons lost. In the spring of 1995, with the TV cameras rolling, "Richard," whose real name is Danny, was taken by his biological father from the only home he had ever known. It was one of the most terrible scenes I've ever witnessed; the child screamed, while the neighbors watched and cried, and Kim Warburton ran sobbing into the house.

As of this writing, a year has passed since the Warburtons lost their son. They, and their other son, eight-year-old Johnny, have never given up hope that Danny will come back to them. They haven't seen or spoken with the child, despite the biological father's promises to arrange regular visits. But, said Kim in a newspaper article, "We never said goodbye to Danny. We said we'd love him forever. Danny is a member of our family and we are just waiting until he comes home." His room is as he left it, complete with his favorite teddy bear.

The family, however, is doing more than simply waiting. The Warburtons are Christians and have started a foundation called kidsHELP! with the intent of bringing together experts to address issues related to adoption, foster care, divorce cases, custody battles, and more—so that, perhaps, other parents and children will be spared the agony the Warburtons have endured. "It's very difficult to step into the future with one foot in the past," Kim admits. But they're trying to turn their pain into something positive.

This is faith. This is perseverance. This, in the words of the young woman I quoted in the introduction, is "seeing Jesus live." It shows how, even *while* we are in the midst of grief, our sorrow can be an agent of healing for others.

The Warburtons aren't spiritual titans any more than the rest of us. "All I know is you limp your way to heaven and get your answers," Kim says.

Not an Answer, but a Person

Which, in the end, is all anyone can do. In heaven my friend will find out why he was never able to find the position for which God seemed to have gifted him so eminently. Barbara Johnson, the author of a number of sad yet funny books about suffering, will be reunited with the sons she lost and will understand the reasons for the pain. In heaven I will badger Jesus with a list of questions the size of an unabridged dictionary. (He'll probably get so weary of my pestering he'll contemplate sending me back: "Oh, I just decided, you didn't die. It was only a deep coma.")

In the meantime—which is so often, it seems, the *mean* time—we're here, and we don't always get it, and our strength can fail us, and things seem to take forever (with the sole exception of one's children growing up), and the outcome isn't always what we expect, so that our response to "hang in there" is often an exasperated, "Okay, now what?"

"Now what"—or who—is God's grace, as revealed in Christ, "God with us," feeling what we feel. I've heard stories about teenage boys with cancer who lost their hair after chemotherapy treatments, and whose friends shaved their heads as a gesture of support. That, in a way, is how Christ comes to us, how he came to us—only he didn't give up his hair, he gave up his life.

"Now what" is Christ—in the hard times, in the good times, in the middling times, in the meantime, and in the time to come. We have his word on it. He said to the Twelve (or, by then, the Eleven) on his last night on earth, "Now is your time of grief, but I will see you again and you will rejoice, and no one will take away your joy" (John 16:22).

And so we limp our way to heaven, perhaps confused, perhaps impatient, perhaps even angry. But what a hope! And in the meantime—God still has some surprises in store, as we shall see.

Chapter Seven

Surprise! God Showed Up!

My daughter and I used to watch the family sitcom *Full House*. Okay, it could get a little syrupy sometimes, but it was entertaining. A little lesson-in-life was usually inserted at the end of the program, and the characters were appealing. One of the minor players was a terminally inarticulate teenage boy, the friend of ubiquitous neighbor Kimmy. (By the way, do you know anyone who is best friends with their next-door neighbors, the way it always is in sitcoms? The only way I know that our next-door neighbors are even alive is because periodically their grass gets mowed or their snow shoveled.) Anyhow, this kid, I think his name was DeWayne, hardly ever talked, but stood around with a goofy grin. His all-purpose response to anything anyone said was a shrug and a mumbled, "Whatever." As in, "DeWayne, do you think you'll finally graduate from high school?" "Heh, whatever."

The other day I read an article in the paper taking Bob Dole to task for his habit of tacking "whatever" onto the end of his sentences. The author sardonically wrote: "Bob Dole will balance the budget, transform welfare as we know it, whatever." The writer thought this indicated sloppy speech on the part of someone who should know better.

Brace Yourself!

In the wake of some surprises in my own life, however, I suspect that both DeWayne and Mr. Dole might be on to something. I've about decided that "whatever" may be one of the most appropriate responses to God, who insists on doing things his way and surprising us—nay, knocking our socks off—in the process. "Okay, God, whatever you decide, whatever you choose. I had thought you were away on a long sabbatical, but then you showed up, and I'll never be the same again!" The "whatever" attitude signals not necessarily mumbling passivity but a *malleability*, an eager openness for God to do his work in our lives. "Whatever, Lord." Or, "Thy will be done."

One of the interesting things about writing a book like this, a book that deals with hurts and joys and life and God, is that you can show God's impact on your life in "real time," as the computer people say—while it's all happening. You, the reader, can, in a sense, move in with me (here, let me move this clutter out of the way so you can sit down) and watch me through my ups and downs. In the last chapter I shared some of my experiences of trudging along like a tortoise, slow and steady, trusting in God. That's been more than an exercise for me lately; I've been waiting for some things to happen, and they haven't been happening and so I've kind of given up worrying about them, because worry eats away at you and makes you negative and unpleasant and people stop inviting you places.

Walking by faith is supremely important. But then, usually out of the blue, Christ decides to appear and walk alongside of you and come to your house.

When the Check Really *Is* in the Mail

A long-lost friend called me late one evening. She had moved West more than a decade before, and our lives had taken separate paths. There wasn't a basis for keeping in touch, like you have automatically through family or a professional connection. I would occasionally think of her and wonder how she was doing, but my wondering wasn't strong enough to nudge me to write her.

She called as she was passing through town on her way back East to make arrangements for her mother's funeral. She told me about her spiritual journey, about how some long-awaited dreams were about to bear fruit, about her serious car accident a couple of years before ("by rights, I should be dead or paraplegic"). She talked about risking and courage and overriding those inner censors that tell us, *You can't.*

It was exactly what I needed to hear, a true godsend from the most unexpected of places. Behold, I am doing a new thing! Do you not see it? (Probably not.) Our conversation motivated me to make some calls the next day, calls I had put off, which is my usual way. Those, too, were encouraging and surprising.

And the same day, I received yet another piece of news. One of my books had "earned out" its advance—the up-front money an author receives from a publisher when she contracts to write a book. Publishers only start paying royalties when the advance money is recouped from sales. This book was the furthest thing from my mind; I was too immersed in current projects. I knew it was out there, still in print, piddling along, but that was all I knew. I never call publishers to check on sales figures. A friend of mine did that once, and after the sales department representative had called up the data on her computer, she said, "Hmm, let's see—oh, dear, this *is* bad news." (Evidently no one had told this person, who theoretically was in charge of author relations, that authors' egos are about as strong as milkweed fluff.)

Turns out the piddling little book has done okay. Not Frank Peretti-blockbuster numbers, but okay when you consider that the vast majority of the fifty thousand titles published every year sink unseen without making a ripple. And a check was in the offing! Cynical me. I'm always sneering about those check-in-the-mail stories, holding them up as the worst example of the God-waving-a-magic-wand mentality. And now . . . well, I'm wondering if that rumble of thunder I just heard wasn't a divine chuckle.

But I hadn't even prayed for this to happen. I had been praying for other things and feeling bad that those other things hadn't turned out the way I hoped. And then God chose to do *this* thing. I was praying for my struggling friends, but God chose to send me *this* friend and, through her struggle, teach me something about trust.

I'm not at all sure that I can infer a connection between *anything* I did and God's action. But I suspect I was watching for the "whatever," so I would know it when I saw it. It's just that I'm not sure I would have looked so hard if things had been great.

What Will God Think of Next?

Remember what Anne Lindbergh said about openness and vulnerability being prerequisites to learning through struggle? I believe that through all the praying and wrestling and wondering, through seeking God's hand and through finally surrendering our will to his, we become more malleable, more attuned to the unseen work of the Holy Spirit. We see God because we really *need* to see God.

I like the way Oswald Chambers expresses it: "When through Jesus Christ we are rightly related to God, we learn to watch and wait, and wait wonderingly. 'I wonder how God will answer this prayer.' . . . 'I wonder what glory

God will bring to himself out of the strange perplexities I am in.'"

Think of Jane Hess Merchant, the poet who suffered from brittle-bone disease. She was without mobility, without hearing, and at times without sight—surely a "strange perplexity!" But she was always, even in her times of depression and inward wrestling, acutely aware of God. Remember what she said? "It isn't superficial with me."

I feel compelled to give equal time to one dear friend who disagrees with me about this. She says she feels alienated from God during hard times and close to him during good times—more conscious of his grace and provisions. Perhaps she's wiser than I, who seem to need that periodic shaking up from on high. At best we can become complacent and self-satisfied when things are going well; at worst, as Billy Graham observes, we can become "callous and unreachable." Wrestling with problems helps us flex our spiritual muscles, gives our faith a hungry edge, and sharpens our vision to seek out whatever God might come up with next.

Zeal Through the Mire

The psalmists knew something about that hunger. Consider, for example, Psalm 69. The psalmist begins with an anguished plea: "Save me, O God, for the waters have come up to my neck. I sink in the miry depths, where there is no foothold. I have come into the deep waters; the floods engulf me. I am worn out calling for help; my throat is parched. My eyes fail, looking for my God" (vv. 1–3).

He continues, describing the scorn and mockery he has endured, the shame he feels, the retribution he wishes God would visit upon his enemies. My study Bible speculates that King David *may* have written the psalm after his adulterous affair with Bathsheba, but that the author could also have been Jeremiah, lamenting the fall of Jerusalem. Either way, this is the cry of a wounded soul. Yet, as in so many of the Psalms and prophetic books, the writer concludes with praise: "The LORD hears the needy and does not despise his captive people. Let heaven and earth praise him, the seas and all that move in them ..." (vv. 33–34).

Then there is this verse, tucked in the middle: "For zeal for your house consumes me ..." (v. 9). What a great word, *zeal*. It carries an intensity that words like *enthusiasm* lack. And the fact that the psalmist is able to proclaim this zeal shortly before he laments, "I am the song of the drunkards" (v. 12, and don't you love the bluntness of Scripture?), amazes me and speaks to the ping-ponging, yes, but internal debates with which many of us struggle.

Out of Exhaustion, New Life

Larry Crabb, in his book *Finding God*, speaks of much the same thing. He uses the term "immobility"—not the physical immobility Jane Merchant experienced, but the worn-out paralysis of the soul that can come to all of us when we realize that some of our longings will never be met, that life will never quite live up to our standards. We cry out to God, but when he does not respond as we wish, we finally yield to exhaustion, unable to exert any energy in solving our problems. And then, says Crabb, something happens: "As exhaustion immobilizes us, as we lose interest in making things better, we are slowly freed to pursue God. We are desperate now not for solutions *from* God, but for fellowship *with* God. . . . As we remain prostrate, without scrambling for a way to revive our spirits enough to stand up and carry on with life, we hear a new voice, faint at first, but clearer and more real than any we've ever before heard."

Gradually, says Crabb, we become more alert to the presence of God. We read the Bible with new appreciation; our prayer lives have new depth; the sacraments take on personal meaning.

This is one way we can learn through suffering. But, as Crabb points out with admirable honesty and from personal experience, the lesson doesn't always stick. Life gets in the way—disappointment, loss, money woes, marital problems, faithless friends, our own awareness of how flawed we are. Sin gets in the way. We go through the whole struggling-and-yielding process again and again—the ping-ponging—but with each struggle, we're drawn a little closer to Christ. "And slowly," says Crabb, "we change."

The hard thing = the best thing.

Looking Back...

While I agree with Larry Crabb in principle, I don't necessarily think it always works this dramatically. (But then, I never believed check-in-the-mail stories, either. So what do I know? Whatever, Lord.) In my own life, I haven't always been aware of one particular moment when I felt myself yielding and then sensed the still, small voice. When I'm *really* in the pits, I don't necessarily feel close to God, and I don't want someone telling me that my misery will make me a better Christian. I don't go saying to the Almighty, "Yes, Lord, thanks for bounced checks and stomach flu. Now, could you please bring back the zits I had when I was fifteen so I can enjoy yet another teachable moment?" I'm not that wise; I see in a mirror dimly. It's in my rearview mirror, once I'm past the worst of things, that I gain a sharper perspective. Through it all, as I've already said, I argue with God, carrying on one-sided monologues like Tevye the dairyman in *Fiddler on the Roof*. But it's a lover's quarrel, a passionate and vulnerable reaching-out. And I believe God reaches back. Believe? I *know* he does.

I used to wonder why so many Christians testified to some experience of God by saying something like, "Looking back, I can see God's hand in. . . ." Why, I would think, *can't* we connect with God more directly while we're in the midst of the struggle? Why do the pieces of the puzzle only seem to come together months or sometimes years later? Wouldn't we be spared a lot of grief if we could immediately understand God's purposes and perhaps correct our course accordingly?

Well, in a way. But there are several reasons, having to do with the nature of God and the nature of us, why we usually can't. Linda, the woman with multiple sensitivities, said she was "too busy trying to survive" during her years of hospitalization to exert much spiritual energy. During our darkest moments, we often feel helpless. Right now, as I've mentioned before, I have this friend who's going through a valley the size of the Mariana Trench. (If you're not up on your geography, that's the deepest hole in the world. It's somewhere in the Pacific, over near Asia.) She's tried and tried and *tried* to understand God's purposes in her struggle. She's sick of people gushing to her, "I just *know* God is going to work a miracle out of this!"

"I keep hearing this, but I'm not so sure," she's confessed to me.

I've written elsewhere about how God gives us more responsibility than we sometimes realize. Like a wise parent, he wants us to learn things for ourselves, sometimes the hard way. Also, "God's purposes" for our lives go way beyond any immediate situation. He sees the whole of our existence, stretching into eternity; considering his perspective, we're like ants looking up at Mt. Everest.

And I think it pleases him when we wake up and say, "Whoa, *now* I get it! I never dreamed that *that's* what you had in mind, Lord!"

Dry Bones and New Blood

Years ago my husband and I were deep in the miry depths to which the above psalmist refers. I've never written about this anywhere because it was so painful, but the outcome testifies to God's goodness. Fritz was pastoring a certain church and, over the course of five years there, we had brought in a lot of new people, many of them young families. It seemed as if we—or God's Spirit—were breathing life into the dry bones of an aging, stagnant body.

Trouble is, some of the old guard resented the new blood. (Those of you involved in church leadership may recognize the syndrome.) They also resented us, and they got some of "their" people on the board. Church board meetings and congregational budget meetings turned into rancorous free-for-alls. If you want to learn about suffering, try sitting through a meeting where they're openly discussing whether your husband "deserves" a raise.

On top of everything else, we had an infant daughter to care for, a gift from God in the midst of trouble. I dimly sensed then—and am certain now—that there were dark forces at work in the situation. Not wanting to expose an innocent babe to the poisonous atmosphere at church, I began staying home Sunday mornings.

Fritz eventually resigned and began looking for a new pastorate. But we didn't feel led to the churches that were interested in him, and the churches we were interested in weren't led to us. We lived in a parsonage, and time was growing short. We would soon have to leave the church, and we had no clue where to go.

Now, you can lose a job, but if you can hang onto your house you have a certain measure of stability, which you especially need if you have children. (This theme of "home" must go deep into my subconscious. I sometimes have dreams in which our family are homeless squatters who sneak into unoccupied houses—often our former parsonage—and spend the night. Then I wake up and am so grateful for our house, as old and small as it is.)

I'd like to say that, during that crisis, I prayed early and often. I'd like to say I searched the Scriptures for clues to the way out of our plight. I'd like to say I met regularly for counsel with a small group of trusted fellow believers.

I'd like to say all this, but the truth is I was a lonely pastor's wife whose closest friend in the church was herself. Even allies in a church fight can form a foxhole sort of bond that dissolves once the battle is over. To be honest, I was too angry and too consumed with immediate survival and with my baby's needs to be able to derive much wisdom from anywhere or anyone.

We finally wound up renting an apartment—a very nice apartment, actually—in a town near where I had worked before Amanda was born. And, slowly, the healing began.

From the Bad News to the Good News

Why did we have to endure all that? What was the *purpose* of my dear husband taking such emotional abuse?

Looking back—there, I've said it—I can see a bunch of reasons. Most particularly, this one: We had always wanted to live in the community we're in now. It was a dream of ours, but we saw no way that it could happen as long as we were still in the pastorate. So we pushed it to the back of the dream drawer like we did with so many other wishes.

Then suddenly, there we were, unloading our rented moving truck in that very same town. I have to grin at the irony. The good news is, you're where you wanted to be. The bad news is, you practically had to get fired to get there.

Stuff like this just keeps happening, whether I've asked for it or not. I'm starting to realize what Oswald Chambers meant about learning to wonder what glory God can bring out of perplexities. I'm almost certain it—*whatever*—won't be what I expect, but I'm absolutely certain it will be what I need.

Chapter Eight

Have Mercy!

I *love* giving advice. I would have made a great Ann Landers. Ask me anything! Parenting problems . . . struggles with unemployment . . . marriage questions . . . what to do with a glut of giant zucchini from the garden. (Send them overseas to some underequipped youth baseball league, perhaps.) If I don't have the answer to your problem, I'll make up something plausible or at least invoke the all-purpose Christian response: "Thank you for sharing that."

My daughter is still young enough that she actually sometimes listens to me. Okay, Amanda, here's how you tackle your homework. Here's how you deal with that friend who dumped you (after I claw the kid's eyes out). I recommend you wear the black pants with the purple top. Not that she always takes my advice, and soon enough she will turn a deaf ear to my well-meaning input, or so I've been warned. I guess I'm sort of loading her up with advice in preparation for those lean years, the way another mom might load up her son with sheets and light bulbs as he leaves for his first bachelor apartment. It's what we mothers do, load up our kids. It's as if we're convinced that if we don't, they'll come back to us some day homeless and starving. Even now, we *never* leave my mother-in-law's house empty-handed—and she's in her seventies.

The Temptation to Fix Others

Now, we can't exactly load up our friends in the same way, and I'm not sure we should, most of the time.

There are those friends of mine in deep need. Kid problems. Health problems. Money problems. Questions about God's goodness. At times I've had to close my mouth against the temptation to say things like, "You really need to make time for yourself so you don't get so frazzled" or "You should take a hard look at your finances" or even "Maybe your struggle is exposing a flaw in your spiritual life, and this is God's way of telling you you need to work on that flaw."

I may be right. I may even be speaking the truth in love. But the truth is, when things get really dark and my friends are reaching out for help, they (and, for that matter, my daughter) need my love more than they need my expertise.

The thing is, it's so easy to solve other people's problems. Even Ann Landers got divorced a few years ago. It's so easy to think we really know what's going on in someone else's life, so easy to be judgmental. Why doesn't he *get* it— if he just stopped spending money on expensive computer equipment, he wouldn't be so broke. Don't they realize that if they just set consistent limits, their kids wouldn't be so out of control? Why does she let her husband push her around in the name of "submitting"? Why don't poor people show some gumption and get off welfare?

But the older I get, the more I realize that people have all kinds of hidden subtexts to their lives, all kinds of limitations and complications beyond my ken. I mean, have you ever wondered why people are messing up, seemingly more than ever, when twenty million blame their lives in the name of publishing many advice mavens are out there that someone could start an ent "The Expert Channel"? (Watch, someo these great ideas, never act on them, and t body making big bucks from the same, usually concept months later.)

So I look at my friend who adopted three kids with various problems. She doesn't need more choice nuggets from my vast store of wisdom, especially when I have one kid who—so far, thank God—has been blessedly easy to rear. Anything I could say, she probably knows already. What she does need—what everyone needs—is a friend to embody the love of Christ to her.

And that, for me, begins with compassion.

We Love, Because He ...

Here's the place for the usual disclaimer that, as Christians, we're called to bring others to obedience and accountability, that Scripture speaks of both law and grace, and that our faith is about more than feel-good platitudes. And yes, Jesus did challenge and probe and rebuke. But underlying his entire life and ministry—even underlying the rebukes—is a heart of infinite compassion: it's why he came to us and why he died for us. For God so loved the world ...

As I read the Gospels I see a Savior who heals, usually without asking questions. I see him welcoming the children, chastising the self-important, allowing his feet to be anointed, bringing a message of hope to the downtrodden. I see him promising his frightened disciples in John 14 that he will leave them a Counselor who will remind them of everything he said while he was among them.

I have received, time and again, his compassion in uggles.

ompassion is more than a bleeding-heart sort of feeling ry for someone. My dictionary defines compassion as "the eep feeling of sharing the suffering of another, together with the inclination to give aid or support or to show mercy."

And mercy springs directly from the heart of God. A letter in *Christianity Today* magazine—interestingly, from a woman I know—said it well. Author Becky Freeman observed that the Lord requires us to "do justly . . . and to *love* mercy. When there's doubt as to which to apply, I'd rather err on the side of excessive mercy. For there, I believe, is where God's heart also leans. It is my *just* Father's *love of mercy* that humbles me, makes me long to walk with him." (Emphases hers.)

We love, because he first loved us. We live out mercy, because he has shown us his mercy. We weep with those who weep, because we have felt the healing rain of Christ's tears. We give to others what we have also received. I like the dictionary definition; compassion isn't just something you feel, it's something you *do*. Give aid and support. Show mercy. There's a "withness" in compassion, a feeling of connection and identification. Compassion doesn't just send a check to the Salvation Army; compassion muses, What must it *feel* like to be an inner-city mother who sends her "babies" off to school every day, wondering if they'll come home in one piece? What must it be like to be a black man who's stopped by the police for no reason?

Compassion is another gift that suffering can bestow, another way that the hard thing is the best thing—*God's* best thing. Scratch a truly merciful person and you'll find some buried wounds, some failures God is using to minister to others.

Ham Salad and Eloquence

Writers, like anyone else, have idols. I saw one of the desks at which C. S. Lewis wrote—it's part of a Wheaton College collection of things Lewisian. I reverently ran my hand over the surface, as if I thought I might pick up some of his genius from the grain, the way a baseball fan might caress Babe Ruth's bat.

I'm also an admirer of Walter Wangerin Jr., who wrote *The Book of God* (Scripture as a great and connected story) and *The Book of the Dun Cow* (up there with the Narnian chronicles, in my estimation) and many other books of story and wisdom. Before I met him, Walt loomed as this Olympian figure in my imagination. Then I went to his house to interview him and his wife, Thanne, for a magazine piece. I rang the doorbell, inwardly quaking and hoping they wouldn't notice. Thanne answered and ushered me into the Holy of Holies . . . I mean, into Walt's study. Then suddenly he appeared, wearing sweats and looking like a regular person. He asked if I was hungry and if I liked ham salad. He has a slightly theatrical voice, so the question, "Do you like ham salad?" sounded more like a catechist asking his catechumens, "What is the chief end of man?" But what a disarming bit of earthiness. Ham salad!

Now that I think about it, he was probably seeking to put me at ease. As we talked, both then and in subsequent meetings, and as I've read his books, my strongest impression of Wangerin is of a man who deeply understands sorrow and mercy and that sense of being *with* those who struggle, rather than judging from above.

It did not surprise me, therefore, when I read in one of his books of his sometimes desperate unhappiness as a schoolboy, of how he was the object of a *Lord-of-the-Flies* sort of cruelty to which children can subject one another. Its sting can last a lifetime, perhaps because the child's mind is so spongelike and receptive. It is a suffering that should *never* be minimized by parents or teachers.

Forrest Gump, Role Model

It would be simplistic to say that Walt Wangerin is a great and sensitive writer because he suffered as a child. Or that Garrison Keillor—another of my favorites, although I've never had the privilege of eating a ham salad sandwich in his home—tells compassionate stories of above-average folks in Lake Wobegon because he was gawky and wore glasses and felt like a misfit growing up. But the mercy is there. The mercy is there in the man I saw on TV who was in a car accident and became paraplegic, and now spends his days ministering to the homeless. The mercy, obviously, is in Barbara Johnson, who, although so greatly grieved, chooses to say to others, "Okay, you're in pain, I'm in pain, we're all in some kind of pain . . . but let's look for the joy and hold on to the Savior."

You've probably seen the movie *Forrest Gump*. Remember how he keeps trying to rescue Jenny? He attempts to save her from a college guy he thinks is trying to assault her in a parked car; he saves her from humiliation as she sings in a seedy bar; he comes to her defense against her scuzzy war-protester boyfriend; he takes her into his house when she, sick from drug addiction, has nowhere to go; and, in the end, he takes in their son after he buries her.

At first I was irritated with sweet, dumb Forrest for pursuing the willfully self-destructive Jenny. I wanted to yell, "Stop wasting your time! She's not good enough for you, boy!" But finally I realized that here was an extraordinary example of mercy—of compassion—in action.

You see, Forrest himself is limited. He had had a hard time of it, growing up slow-minded. But instead of pitying himself, he chose to devote much of his time to helping others. He took over his slain Vietnam buddy's shrimping business; he rescued the disabled lieutenant from a skid row half-life.

It should not be surprising that Forrest himself had also received a gift: His mother had always believed in him and fought for him. He gave, because he received.

Go and Tell!

And so it is with those of us who struggle. We remember what Christ has done for us.

Recall the story of Jesus healing the demon-possessed man in the region of the Gerasenes. After Jesus sends the demon into the swine, he gets into the boat and the man begs to go with him. "Jesus did not let him, but said, 'Go home to your family and tell them how much the Lord has done for you, and how he has had mercy on you.' So the man went away and began to tell in the Decapolis how much Jesus had done for him. And all the people were amazed" (Mark 5:19–20).

Much of this book has been born out of my desire to share how the Lord has had mercy on me; how he has, time and again, shown me his patience and faithfulness and his kind of love that will not let go. He has rescued me from my sinfulness and willfulness, and as we saw in the last chapter, he has challenged me and guided me and continually surprised me. Even as a searching prodigal in my college years, I sensed he was waiting to welcome me home. I can echo what Oswald Chambers observes: "The more complicated the actual conditions are, the more delightfully joyful it is to see God open up his way through."

There but for…

When we understand our own frailties, we're more likely to be gentle toward others in their frailties. We're less likely to succumb to the sin of pride—the sin, as C. S. Lewis suggested, that is "the complete anti-God state of mind."

In *The Grace Awakening*, Charles Swindoll talks about the downside of the pursuit of such seeming strengths as excellence, discipline, education, and independence. The flip side of the pursuit of excellence, he says, is intolerance. A disciplined lifestyle can bring about "impatience and the tendency to judge" others. An educated appreciation for culture and the arts can make a person a snob. And someone who pulls himself up by his bootstraps, accepting no handouts, can be prideful.

How alien to the idea that all good gifts—all handouts, if you will—come from the "Father of the heavenly lights" (James 1:17)!

When friends and family make a big deal about my having written a few books, I kind of shrug it off. Yes, I've pursued excellence in my craft (what you're reading represents about the eighth revision of this paragraph); yes, I try to work with some semblance of discipline. But I'm also aware that I've received a lot of mentoring along the way; that I come from two creative parents; and that I've been given the gift of work I enjoy (and I can sit at home in my jammies and do it).

I've made some wise choices (my life's partner among them), but I've also made some poor choices and experienced some crashing disappointments. There's a lot I could do better. Life hasn't necessarily come that easy for me. Life doesn't come that easy for most of us, even though it may look that way on the surface for some people. And those parts that do come easy aren't necessarily to our credit.

Compassion looks at the struggler and says, "That could be me. That *is* me."

So I want to extend to others a fraction of the grace— the mercy—Christ has extended to me.

"I Didn't Want to Hurt Her Feelings"

I look at my daughter, growing so rapidly. Almost a teenager, going to middle school next year! She's one of these superkids (said the mother modestly)—blonde and beautiful, bright enough to be in gifted programs, athletic and well-liked.

But what pleases me most, apart from the commitment to Christ she made at an early age, is the fact that Amanda is, with exceptions I shall refer to presently, growing into a compassionate young person. She'll say things to me like, "I didn't say anything because I didn't want to hurt her feelings." The pain of the world is starting to weigh on her. The other night as she was getting ready for bed, she began to ask those where-is-God-when-it-hurts? questions. "If God is so good, why are people homeless?" she asked, with some heat. "Why are people shot coming home from birthday parties?" (I don't know where *that* came from.) "Why doesn't he always answer prayers?"

Lest you think she's one of these too-perfect-to-believe Christian kids, I will also point out that not long ago, as she came out of the Wheaton College snack bar with her dad and saw a boy from school, she curled her lip and went "Eeewww" to his face. "Mom, *nobody* likes him," she told me when I chided her later. "And he starts it, because he's mean. I would never be mean for no reason." Apparently boys, for the moment, are exempt from her benevolence. (Maybe just as well.)

But the unfortunate lad may be the exception that proves the rule: my child sorrows for others. Has she sorrowed

herself to become softened in this way? Perhaps. A part of
me would like to have it otherwise; I long to smooth the way
for her and spare her from hurt. And yet I know that in that
way lies arrogance and unkindness, that the fruit of the Spirit
is nourished by the wind and the rain. I want her to marvel at
God opening his way through.

The amusing thing is that I already see Amanda evinc-
ing some of the same know-it-all, advice-giving impulses
that seize me from time to time. (Not surprising, really; her
dad is the same way, as are various kin on both sides of our
family tree. We're kind of an opinionated bunch.)

Of course, there are times when the kind thing, the gen-
erous thing, is to share a few *very* carefully chosen words.
But I would hope that her words . . . and mine . . . would
come cloaked in compassion—the same compassion that
we sense when we feel the breath of the Master's presence.

I would hope, too, that that same breath would lift us
and propel us to do more than speak, that it would put feet
on our mercy—something we shall see in the next chapter.

Chapter Nine

Angels and Kids and Mismatched Chairs

Have you ever seen those "Family Circus" cartoon strips where Billy, the eldest boy, goes on his merry way, as boys do, while a gauzily drawn guardian angel saves him from various near disasters, such as stepping into the path of an oncoming car? Billy can't see the angel, who has (of course) a motherly looking face, but we can.

It's a comforting idea, but this business of angels . . . what to think? It bothers me that some people seem to invoke the presence of celestial beings without acknowledging the Source of those beings. Angels appear frequently in the Bible, of course, but I'm not certain about the idea that each of us has his own personalized guardian angel that follows us around and rescues us. But just today, as I prepared to sit down to work, I had a fairly weird experience that made me wonder . . .

I had just made some fresh coffee, and I guess I was excited about the bright spring day (it's been like the monsoon season around here), or maybe I was happy about my coffee (hey, 'tis a gift to be simple), or maybe I was eager to get down to business. Anyhow, my workspace is in our converted back porch off the kitchen, and there's a step down into it. I wasn't paying much attention to where I was going, as can happen when one is so familiar with a certain terrain. I stepped on the threshold between one room and the next and my foot failed to land squarely on the step, but overshot it so that I lost my balance and *almost* went crashing into the bookcase against the opposite wall.

But I didn't. And I don't know why.

There's a real possibility I could have sprained my ankle. The bookshelves could have come crashing down on me. I could have spilled hot coffee on myself. All the laws of inertia point to a nasty fall. I would have failed to finish this book, would have missed various events coming up in this busy end-of-school season, and may have had to postpone our family vacation. Not to mention the nuisance and expense of a trip to the emergency room.

No, I didn't feel invisible hands gripping me. (I don't especially *want* to feel invisible hands gripping me, even though I could probably turn it into a best-selling book.) But somehow I got righted.

Here, speculation can run rampant. If I do have a guardian angel, what does he or she look like? As I recall, in the particular Christian novel I read, the guy's angel was a burly, bearded fellow with a booming voice, something like the Spirit of Christmas Present in Dickens' *A Christmas Carol*. On the other hand, Jimmy Stewart's guardian angel in *It's a Wonderful Life* was named Clarence and looked like . . . well, like a Clarence. I can imagine my angel looking and sounding like, say, James Earl Jones, or perhaps like my Girl Scout leader, Mrs. Redlich, who was comforting and a little stout and understood that eleven-year-old girls are freaked out about having to use latrines in the middle of the night. If I have a guardian angel, does he or she also have charge over other people, maybe all the other insecure evangelical

Christian writers? Or does each of us have just one, kind of how we all have a PIN at the automatic teller?

God's Requirement

Jokes aside, I don't know what I think about guardian angels. But I'm willing to concede the possibility that someone was there to catch me—as Someone has always been there to catch me, as I hope I can be there for others when they stumble. Some things are just too good to keep to yourself. And—more often than not—"angels" can appear under some fairly noncelestial guises.

After my almost-fall I went outdoors and picked some lilies of the valley from the patch that borders our driveway. I love their fragrance and their delicate, scalloped little bells; I keep intending to dig up a clump and move them to a shady spot in front of the house where they can spread and people who walk by can enjoy their fragrance. I thought about Jesus' advice to "consider the lilies of the field." I'm not sure what sort of "lilies" he was referring to, but it's hard to imagine that lilies of the valley, which like shade and cool dampness, would thrive in Galilee. I listened to the birds chirping and remembered what Jesus said about God's care for the sparrows—and for us.

It's true. I've lived it, I've received it, and I want to pass it on to others.

One thing I've come to realize is that the Bible may help you understand life, but life also helps you understand the Bible. We can't fully comprehend the awesomeness of God's promises until the time comes when we really need to hang onto those promises and they become real and touchable and immediate. We may wonder at Jesus' harshness toward the Pharisees until something happens and we realize we're acting just like those smug religious know-it-alls.

And when God sends us these lessons, he wants us to do something with them. To paraphrase Oswald Chambers, you can't accept God's gift and ignore his requirement.

A few chapters ago I spoke of telling painful birth stories and the desire to testify to God's goodness. But there's another step: to bear witness not only through telling, as important as that is, and not only through feeling compassion, but through *acting*, through the giving of ourselves to serve, to help—to heal. And, at least as important, to receive those gifts from others who may themselves be angels with wounded wings.

Ready or Not

I used to think that before I reached out to others, I had to be complete within myself, all problems solved, and wearing a size six to boot. It's a little like our house. For a long time I didn't want to entertain visitors because our house isn't Martha Stewart perfect. Our dining room chairs don't match, for instance. Oh, we started out our married life with matching seating, but then the upholstery got kind of grungy and the crosspieces or whatever you call them fell out and . . . oh, never mind. So over time we've acquired various chairs. Some of our friends from church have huge, baronial dining rooms with something like twelve matching chairs, and when you eat there you expect some minion to triumphantly bring in a boar's head on a platter. Our dining room is all right, but it isn't baronial.

And then our house is also small. It has peeling patches on the kitchen ceiling and various other flaws that in my mind have grown into hideous eyesores that no one can possibly miss. But I like to cook and I like people, and Amanda's an only child, so somewhere along the line I decided that my qualms were ridiculous and if I waited until my house was perfect before extending hospitality, our friends would all require special bland diets and a wheelchair ramp up to the front door. We still have to bring in a motley assortment of chairs to accommodate everyone in the dining room, and I still have to pull the shower curtain to hide the hard-water stain in the tub, but so what? We have fun, and nobody goes away hungry.

In the same way, when I began speaking, I developed a message about friendship and loneliness. At first I thought, *Why would people want to hear from someone who's struggled so much with this issue?* But as I told stories about my struggles, the audience would laugh, because they'd been there. I think it made more of an impact than if I had presented myself as one smooth and unbroken by life—as Billy Graham says, as if I had been "set apart, untouched, like a piece of fine china in a locked cabinet."

What could be more moving than listening to Christopher Reeve speak between breaths from his ventilator? What if he—or Joni Eareckson Tada—had waited until they could walk before beginning their work on behalf of the disabled? What if Dave Dravecky only boasted about his pitching exploits and never mentioned his cancer? Or remember Dave Roever, who was injured in Vietnam? In his interview, he told the host that the last time he had appeared on the program, several years ago, he was still contemplating suicide, still in the midst of the emotional fire *while* he was speaking of God to others.

How costly. How Christlike.

What if Paul never spoke of his sins or boasted of his weakness? What if the Gospels never spoke of Peter's denial of Christ?

We struggle. Christ touches us through our pain. We then, out of the overflow of our gratitude, go on to touch

others. We give as much out of our redemption from pain
as we give out of the pain itself.

Out of the Pain, a Church

It's fascinating to watch the transformation of the disciples in Scripture. We think a lot about *Jesus'* suffering on his
last night, but consider how the disciples must have felt. I
picture them in the Upper Room, breaking bread with Jesus
on his last night, scared about the future, wondering why
Judas had fled and what he was up to (and how did the
Master know?). I think of Peter and the others, falling
asleep at Gethsemane. The Bible does not tell us their
response to Jesus' entreaties, but I imagine them waking and
groggily thinking, *Can't we do anything right? Here it is, the
Rabbi's last night on earth, and we doze off and leave him alone when he
told us to watch and pray.*

Peter, especially, must have experienced incredible
agony after he denied his Lord. But this same Peter was
empowered to stand up before the assembly on the day of
Pentecost and, in the name of Christ, urge those present to
"Repent and be baptized!" According to Luke, about three
thousand accepted the call (Acts 2:41). This same Peter
healed a crippled beggar (Acts 3). I wonder what those who
only knew him as a cantankerous fisherman would have
thought if they had seen him speaking to the astonished
onlookers in Solomon's Colonnade!

Permit me another speculation on Scripture, a sort of
"Where Are They Now?" follow-up. Think of all those Jesus
healed from suffering, either physical or emotional—the
blind beggar, Jairus's daughter, the Gerasene boy possessed
by demons, the paralytic whose friends lowered him
through the roof, the Samaritan woman at the well, the
woman caught in adultery, the lepers, and our friend, the

woman with the twelve-year hemorrhage. Have you ever wondered what happened to them? Did they all just go back home and resume their ordinary lives? Or were some of them moved to leave their flocks and nets and families and minister to others as they had been ministered to? Were some of them among the believers who "were together and had everything in common" (Acts 2:44)?

God wants us to do something with what he has given us, both through darkness and sunshine. He doesn't want us to just sit around and feel good about ourselves while others may not be feeling so great.

Laundry and Hope

Every now and then you hear a story that actually gives you hope for this old world. Kenneth Johnson of Washington, D.C., a single African-American man in his fifties, got to thinking about the problems of the youth in his neighborhood and decided he could help. First, he signed up to be a foster parent. Then he adopted five children, including twins. He doesn't have a large house or lavish income, but he says God has given him enough and he wants to share it. The children, shown on TV, were neat, well-dressed, courteous, and diligent students; the house attractive and orderly. Relaxing at the end of a long day, Johnson mused that the biggest challenge he faced as a parent was "keeping up with the laundry."

Oh, and by the way, Johnson was wounded in a robbery in 1981—the event that moved him to think about what he could do for others. He, too, is an angel with a broken wing.

A Child Shall Lead Them

I remember a certain child who is now with the angels. She was born with multiple handicaps—a small brain, unable to walk or speak, nearly blind, often ill. To the world, a child like Mandy is an inconvenience, a financial drain, an example of a meaningless life, a mere "existence."

As usual, the world doesn't get it. Neither did I, when I first learned of her disabilities. I thought, *How awful for her parents, not to have a healthy baby. How tragic and exhausting. What kind of a future will she ever have?*

Then, less than two years after he brought her into the world, God lifted Mandy into his arms, saying, "My child, I'm taking you to a place where you can run and laugh, where, someday, you will be able to see your mother's face clearly and put your arms around her." Her memorial service was packed to overflowing with people—people who wanted to stand with the family in their time of bereavement, but also people whom Mandy had touched. Her parents and sisters gave moving testimonies to Mandy's life and what it had meant. The pastor spoke on the child's absolute helplessness, and how her life was a picture of the utter dependence God wants from us. Others told extraordinary stories of how they were brought to the Lord through Mandy. I remember one particular story of a hospital nurse who saw angels in Mandy's room. Her parents, Marshall and Susan, were visibly worn out. Who wouldn't be? But in their weariness there was a dignity and an eloquence beyond words. Mandy's life had transformed an entire church family.

One child. One child who could hardly sit up and had to wear glasses and never was able to call her parents by name. Hers, a meaningless existence? I don't know if Mandy's parents realize the gift they gave so many of us, both that day and during her life. I know I, who once valued intellect above all else, will never think of a handicapped child in quite the same way again.

Sometimes, then, God uses us as angels unaware. But use us he does. Strength made perfect in weakness. Learning to give . . . and also learning to receive.

Being the "Footwashee"

Learning to receive is, perhaps, a related gift of struggle. Many of us are quite competent when it comes to helping others, to serving others. But when we are forced to sit back and, in effect, let our feet be washed, to allow someone to pour their expensive perfume all over us—it seems embarrassing, almost demeaning. We may not want to feel obligated. Or maybe we're sick of talking about our ongoing problem.

"Here we are again, on the receiving end," a friend lamented not long ago, referring to help she was getting from others in her church. I understood what she meant. I've often felt the same way, as if there were a sort of "neediness chain," with wealthy and benevolent helpers at the top and perpetually struggling souls at the bottom. But when I asked another woman about that, a mother whose children have all kinds of problems, she just laughed and said, "Oh, I got over *that* a long time ago." We even got to laughing about her family serving the important "at least we're not" function—as in, "We may have problems, but 'at least we're not' as bad off as the Smiths." (There's that grace-full humor again!)

This woman has learned, maybe been forced to learn, to give others the gift of her helplessness—as the child Mandy did. She can allow others to stretch themselves, maybe even inconvenience themselves, in service to her and her family.

A while back, a certain commercial for an investment company proclaimed, "Be your own rock." The spots were great, especially the one that showed an elderly black woman piloting a boat through a place that looked like the Everglades. The sentiment was very much in tune with the currently fashionable idea that nobody's going to take care of us, so we've got to take care of ourselves, and become morally purer by doing so.

Well, I'm not so sure. I guess I think we've got to take care of each other, out of our strength and out of our fragility, giving and receiving, serving and being served, reaching out with our wounded wings. This is how the Body, at its best, functions: "All the believers were together and had everything in common. Selling their possessions and goods, they gave to anyone as he had need" (Acts 2:44–45).

And who doesn't, at some time, have need? Who isn't obligated to the One in whose name we're called to do these things?

So now, I think I'm going to invite some people over. I may even tell them the story about my angel.

Chapter Ten

Not "Why" But "Who"

Remember my daughter's questions, "If God is good, why are there homeless? If God is good, why do I have zits?" She has this predilection for asking profound theological questions right at bedtime. Another night she asked, "What if Jesus comes back to Earth and he comes to a place where nobody lives? What if you were on the moon when he comes back? What would it look like from space?" (Boy, there's a scenario for Christian fiction. I bet C. S. Lewis never thought of *that* one.) Still another: "Are Jesus and God the same? If Jesus has always been, was he in the Garden of Eden when Eve ate the fruit? And why is there sin?"

"Perhaps so God could show his power by sending his Son," I replied.

"Couldn't Jesus just make sure that everything *stayed* good?" my Talmudic scholar countered.

"Well, um . . ." Can I go now? (By this time I'm thinking of locking her in with our pastor for an hour's interrogation. Pastor John won't know what hit him.)

It reminds me of a cartoon I saw once. A husband and wife are sitting having a nice picnic when suddenly their son comes tearing up to them, pursued by a cloud of insects. The man says, "Uh-oh. Get ready for the question, 'Why did God make mosquitoes?'"

I myself have often pondered the same thing, especially this spring when our area has been deluged by rain and experts are predicting possibly the worst mosquito invasion ever. It seems excessive, out of whack. I could see a few mosquitoes as food for birds and bats and frogs, but why so *many*? Why do I see millions of mosquitoes, but only a couple of Baltimore orioles a year? It reminds me of something Annie Dillard once wrote about nature being blindly, almost malevolently, fecund. Don't tell *me* about ecological balance.

Well, the Mosquito Question is another of those inquiries to be filed away and taken up to heaven. I have this image of a weary God getting so sick of the question that, when newcomers arrive at the Throne, an angel standing by hands them a printed card with the response.

Not Up *There*, but Down *Here*

But God isn't just sitting back, watching us scratch and slap ourselves. He isn't just up *there*, twiddling his thumbs until he decides to return to Earth. He doesn't leave Amanda—or me, or you—blundering in the dark asking our plaintive questions.

We've spoken of the "gifts of struggle," the profound ways hard times can help shape us. We've talked about qualities of character, lessons, insights. But in the end, the most important gift isn't a quality—it's a Person. The most profound response to the question of "Why do such awful things happen?" is embodied in that same Person; it's to learn about him and to understand deeply and intimately how he comes to us.

I wrote a Good Friday play for our church once. Exercising author's privilege, I cast myself as Mary. The drama was organized around a sort of "stations of the Cross"—chains, wood, nails, thunder, darkness—all those tangible reminders of what it was really like that day we killed God. And so I dressed in a robe and sat at my station, fingering these huge, spiky nails. I spoke of what it was like to be the mother of God, but also to be the mother of a son, and to watch that son die, and how I lingered after the execution because I didn't want to leave him. "I was his mother," I concluded, "and a mother doesn't leave her son."

As I spoke these things, tears began raining down my cheeks. Not artificial actor tears, but real weeping. Poor Jesus. Poor us.

Blessed us!

Here is what Oswald Chambers says: "Consider bare-spirited the tragedy of God, and instantly the energy of God will be upon you." Chambers had such a daring way with words: *tragedy* and *energy* in the same sentence. What? Out of tragedy can come energy? Yes, but not in the way we think. Next to the tragedy of God—taking on the sin and mess of the world, *our* sins and *our* mess, all the way to the Cross—our "tragedies" appear pallid indeed.

And yet, because he can identify with us, they aren't unimportant to him.

Another Teenage Birth

I want to backtrack for a moment from the blood of Calvary to the birth-blood of Christmas. There's something unutterably powerful in thinking that God made himself small and seemingly insignificant. He could have made it cleaner, just *materialized*, full-blown, say, in the Temple courts. But he came into the world through a birth canal, slippery and red. There was an umbilical cord, which carpenter Joseph had to snip. There was a placenta. Mary had to push and moan. And just as those teenagers giving birth at Chicago's Cook County Hospital, which is crowded with the poorest of the poor, would never make the news, this was just another birth to another young Galilean woman. Just another baby, a crying infant who needed to nurse and whose diapers—or the first-century Palestinian equivalent—needed changing. Even in his first minutes, he was experiencing what every baby went through.

I don't quite understand it. I don't think anyone really does. Even one of those early church councils that hammered out the cornerstones of the faith hedged a bit, declaring Jesus "fully God and fully man." And where understanding fails, awe begins—awe and the paradox of worship and relationship.

This is God's response to us and our suffering. He *does* know how it feels, because he was here. My study Bible says he "endured the frustrations of the flesh while living in a sinful world." I'm not sure we always think hard about what that means. We like to think about a strong, sure, confident Jesus—the handsome Christ in all those nice Sunday school pictures. And so he was (although, if you follow Isaiah 53, "handsome" is open to question).

But Jesus was also a man. He *must* have sometimes become discouraged. I picture him going to the synagogue at Nazareth at the beginning of his earthly mission. They knew him there; they might have thought him a bit unusual, having wandered off in Jerusalem when he was twelve—and he seemed to *think* a lot. (He probably badgered Joseph with some of the same questions Amanda asks me.) But he was Joseph's son, and Joseph was well-respected in the community, even though speculation had always swirled around the family concerning some odd events.

So Jesus took his turn in the synagogue reading the Scripture. One time he announced to the men, "I am he of whom the prophet was speaking." The congregation was outraged. *This* man? I wonder if this bothered him a bit, being rejected by people who had known him since boyhood, people he had worshiped with and maybe played games with and studied the Law with. I wonder if he ever became frustrated with the disciples' obtuseness. At times, in the Gospels, you can hear it: "Don't you understand? Don't you get it?"

If Jesus hit his thumb with a hammer while he was doing carpentry work, it would have hurt—just like it hurts my friend Tom the Handyman when *he* accidentally hits his finger with a hammer as he works on our roof. Jesus and the disciples walked everywhere, sometimes distances that would seem unimaginably long to us today, like hiking from Chicago to Milwaukee. His feet were probably desert-toughened, but still, they must have wearied. Maybe the human side of him felt twinges of annoyance at the endless besieging of the crowds.

We know that Jesus loved Lazarus and wept when told Lazarus had died. I'm especially touched by the idea that Jesus had special friends in Lazarus and Mary and Martha; these weren't just nameless followers or objects of his teaching, but friends in whose home he could relax, enjoy conversation, and rest. Martha probably bustled about wanting to pamper Jesus: "Lord, sit. You look tired, and I know you haven't been eating right. Let me bring you some bread I just baked, and fish. Olives, maybe? Dates? I have some nice figs." Maybe Jesus and Lazarus discussed the latest news on the Zealot unrest and how Rome, her patience wearing thin, had sent a new governor to keep the unruly province in line.

Jesus' followers were in the minority. Even though he drew large crowds, I wonder whether some of those who followed him were merely curious. Most people in Palestine *didn't* follow him—it would take three more centuries for the tide to turn. The world knew him not. Did the human side of him ever brood about this?

Jesus—human. Just like us. And yet completely unlike us, unlike us so we could become more like him. Friend—and yet God. Conqueror—and sacrificial lamb.

Here, Let Me Do That for You

It's something of a mystery, this notion of what Christian doctrine calls the "substitutionary atonement"—meaning, in plain words, we did wrong and he suffered so we wouldn't have to. Kids are taught this in Sunday school very early on: Jesus died for all the children. Maybe if Jesus were in the woods with us he'd offer a mosquito his arm so we wouldn't get bitten.

It knocks me over to think that when my strength gives out, there's Jesus, taking my burden upon himself. God hurt so I wouldn't have to. I don't know about you, but I find that comforting beyond words. And, when we suffer, says my wise spiritual guide John Benson, God feels *worse* than we do. His Spirit, according to Paul, "groans" on our behalf.

But there's a lot more going on in the heavenly precincts: "For this reason he had to be made like his brothers in every way, in order that he might become a merciful and faithful high priest in service to God, and that he might make atonement for the sins of the people. Because he himself suffered when he was tempted, he is able to help those who are being tempted" (Heb. 2:17–18).

Not only that, the writer of Hebrews goes on to say, but he's interceding on our behalf (7:25). Jesus prays for us when we cannot or will not—when our words run out, when our strength fails, when we become skeptical about promises that perhaps seem a little worn after hearing them so many times.

Jesus had to become like us so he could mediate before God on our behalf. It reminds me of some ambassador to a country whose culture is radically different from ours— someplace in Asia, perhaps—who comes back and says to the president, "Now I understand why those people act the way they do. I've lived among them, eaten their food, worn their native costume, abided by their mores."

The Cold You Don't Catch

This is all a mystery too great for complete comprehension. With a nod to Philip Yancey, an imperfect analogy from the human body might help. Let's say I go to the supermarket where I pick up a bunch of broccoli to examine it, making sure the heads are tight and a good bluish-green. What I don't know is that a microbe is lurking on the package, courtesy of the last shopper to pick up the vegetable. The microbe is only too glad to jump onto my hand, which is warmer and damper and provides a nurturing environment. Later, I take a free sample of a little cheese square on a stick and pop my hand into my mouth. Now the microbe is really happy. Down the chute it goes, into my bloodstream, ready to camp out on a vulnerable cell. Meanwhile, I've returned home, completely unaware of this new threat.

But my antibodies, T cells and IgA and IgG and all the other good guys, have sensed the intruder and rally to defend my system. They swallow up the microbe, which never had a chance.

How many times, I wonder, has Jesus' intervention gone similarly unnoticed by me? The annoyance that could have blown up into a crisis but didn't, the mistake not made, the hurtful words left unsaid—even without my praying or thinking about them. Christ is always there, saving me from myself.

In the Meantime ...

And yet people do get sick and suffer and die, every day. My dad was pumped full of antibiotics as he battled pneumonia, but eventually his exhausted system was overwhelmed and God brought his suffering to an end. The Enemy is still among us, walking to and fro over the earth. Some microbes, apparently, have become smart, adapting to antibiotics and raising the specter of an infectious outbreak that could rage out of control. Immune systems can turn traitorous—ask those with AIDS.

Sometimes God lets me make costly mistakes. As long as we live in this in-between time, between Christ's coming to earth and his return, God's work isn't quite complete. We are a chosen race, but we are also a fallen race. As Philip Yancey puts it, we're living on Easter Saturday.

But while we wait, Jesus has left his Spirit to dwell within us, to encourage and equip us until he comes again.

I see his Spirit strongly at work in Paul's letter to the Philippians. It makes me feel better about myself. I know, I know, that's supposed to be a shallow desire. But his epistle reassures me that even in the midst of struggle, even against the backdrop of this world's unfairness, I have the opportunity to move a bit closer to Christ, to become a bit more like him, if I "live up to what [I] have already attained" (3:16).

Paul *doesn't* promise a world where virtue is always rewarded, where Christians never divorce, and where children don't get leukemia. In fact, Paul himself was under house arrest when he wrote to the Philippians, and the mad

Nero was on the imperial throne. Only through the agency of the Spirit could he make such ringing affirmations as "Whatever is true . . ."

And only through the agency of Christ's Spirit can I rise above my natural tendencies toward apathy and laziness and irritation. Only through his Spirit could Scott and Patricia Willis, a pastor and his wife who lost six children in a car accident, stand in front of the TV cameras with their burn-scarred faces and speak of God's goodness and their anticipation of seeing their children in heaven.

In the very dance of struggle, in the questioning and hurting, in the surrendering and the attempts to take back, in the efforts to "get better" and in the dull disillusionment when you feel you're not getting better and never will, in the urgent paging through Scripture to seek a word that speaks to your plight, in the reaching out to others, and in the thirst to find the good and the better and the best—in these Christ draws us closer to him. And he may, through this process, give us a glimpse of what our souls long for.

Mrs. Holmquist's Opus

Eventually, what seems so all-consuming right now won't matter. Because Christ was raised, frail flesh will give way to a glorified and resurrected body. There will be no more pain, ever, and Jesus will be waiting for us.

Most of us are too caught up in the swirl of this life to see through to anything else. What we're going through seems like an eternity. Occasionally, though, if we're watching closely, we might get a peek behind the fog. When my husband's grandmother, a lifelong woman of God, was ninety, she had to go into a nursing home. Up until then she had always managed in her own home, a rambling Victorian with some exquisite furniture and seven pianos and assorted organs where she taught music well into her eighties. We always agreed that God must have been taking special care of Congi, as her grandkids called her (her full name was Ragnhild Holmquist Congdon, Rae for short), because she was somewhat inattentive to minor details like house wiring and was likely to have bunches of extension cords running under carpets and feeding into one outlet. But she managed, making great Swedish meatballs and presiding over her home like a tiny *grande dame* until her tenth decade. We have some remarkable photos of her at our wedding, holding court in a fur stole and sparkly orange gown.

But she had some worrisome falls. She grew frailer until, regretfully, her children decided it was time for Rae to live in a place where she could be cared for.

I visited her there once. I don't remember now if she was awake; she may have been dozing as the very old doze. She had always been little; now she was almost weightless, a tiny, rustling husk. I remember white. Her hair, which had always been carefully dressed (and, so my husband thinks, tinted), was now white and wispy. She may have been wearing a white sweater. The bed was white.

What I saw in this very old lady was the wearing away of the flesh and the emergence of the spirit. It was as if she already had one size-four foot in eternity and was about to bustle in and tell the angel choirs, "No, no! Sing over the bridge! It must come out of the top of the head!"

Rae slipped away not long after that. My husband, newly ordained, prayed at her funeral. We sang hymns she loved. A good life and—as much as possible—a good death. But I knew that the good-byes weren't permanent. Through this marvelous woman, I had glimpsed a sliver of light shining through a crack in the Door. Now she's up there with C. S. Lewis and his wife, Joy, and baby Mandy, who once was blind but now sees, and Mandy's little brother Toby, and my dad and my husband's dad and all the slaves who sang "Swing low, sweet chariot, coming for to carry me home." (Rae's probably telling *them* how to sing, too.)

It's a song of promise and comfort and eternal hope, a song of welcome and laughter, a song of homecoming and of gratitude, to the God-in-Christ who was there before us, is there with us, and will be there forever.

Now that's something to look forward to.

Chapter Eleven

Morning by Morning, New Mercies...

Remember when we started out, how I talked about the robins in the sleet and crocuses in the snow? Well, the snow and sleet are long gone and so are the crocuses—but the robins are still here.

Today is the first day of summer. A June bug got in our house the other night. (I'm sensing a recurring subtext here.) You think Amanda's freaked out about mosquitoes—have you ever seen an eleven-year-old girl cower in a fetal position? (Why wasn't I getting rid of the thing? That is why God created husbands. I've always wondered how single parents deal with bugs.)

The lawn needs cutting. (That is why God created . . .) The garden needs weeding. I have only three T-shirts I really like. We have wall-to-wall carpeting, and in the humidity it takes on a sort of Eau de Wet Dog scent. Yes, we have central air, but to run it requires one of those crossroads decisions: Do we crank up the AC, thereby ensuring a monster electric bill, or do we eat? As for me and my house, we're rather partial to eating. This coming weekend we're helping some friends move. The temperature is supposed to reach ninety-four, and all the TV news shows will air horrible stories about some elderly person who died in a suffocating apartment.

I love summer when it's idyllic, like every single summer in my childhood was. We had one such evening like this recently. We had just put in our tomato and pepper plants, slapping and scratching all the while, and had rewarded ourselves by sitting on the porch with orange-juice-and-lemonade concoctions. The lawn was green and smooth, the westering sun slanted over the lushly leaved trees, the seductive scent of mock orange drifted over from the neighbor's bush. Some acquaintances stopped by with Silver, their beautiful Siberian husky. They complimented us on how nice the yard looked. I preened. We patted the bumptious, friendly dog.

Who drank my drink.

I had left it on the ledge next to me. Next thing I know, here's this creature with the blood of ancient wolves coursing through her veins lapping up a tall cool one. (I thought dogs like that lived off of caribou meat or something.) "Heh heh," I said, and hastened to reassure Silver's owners it was just fruit juice.

If the mosquitoes don't spoil your party, White Fang will.

In Praise of Winter

So summer has its, well, limitations. There are times when winter starts to look pretty good. No bugs. No yard guilt. Sweaters. Beef stew. Winter at its most beautiful is fierce and cleansing and silence-inducing. In fact, in recent years we've had really wimpy winters—a couple of snows and that's it. I want a foot of snow, drifts on which you can climb and play King of the Mountain, ice-necklaced trees, howling winds. I want a winter like it seems it always was when I was a kid and my dad would tie our saucer sled to the back of the car. We'd take turns sitting on the sled while he drove around our icy, little-traveled circular road. We'd hang onto the sled for dear life, squealing as we rounded the turns that sometimes dumped us into snowbanks. (I know it probably sounds like my dad was trying to get rid of us, but trust me, it was all in good fun.)

I want to stand outside deep in January when it seems as if the world will never wake from its sleep; when even the noisy crows, who always remind me of strutting bouncers at gambling casinos, have retreated into the protection of the spruces. I want to look up at a purply-blue sky and wonder at Orion striding across the heaven with Sirius, the Dog Star, yapping at his heels. I want to see Queen Cassiopeia lounging on her W-shaped throne and find Taurus the Bull, ready to charge. It's funny . . . apart from the Big Dipper, I'm virtually clueless when it comes to summer constellations. I can be out of doors on a warm, gentle night and have no idea what I'm looking at. Put me outside in winter, though, and I might die of hypothermia, but I'll do it pointing upward at the stars.

When I get to heaven, I'm going to ask God why he put all the best and clearest constellations in the winter sky. (I hope I remember all of these questions when the time comes.) Maybe he wanted us to work a little harder to discover them. Sometimes real treasure takes some digging to get to.

I want to listen to winter's deep silence, so different from that of summer. It's never truly quiet in summer, even out in the country. There's always the underlying rustle of crickets and the wind riffling the leaves and perhaps a mouse scurrying through the grass—there's a kind of thickness in the air. But in midwinter, on a really cold night, you can almost hear the air snap. Even the moon looks forbidding.

I've grown to love winter because it displays the raw, stripped-bare elements of God's power. God brings light and warmth and green in its season, but then he puts everything to sleep and brings the darkness. Once, around the time of the winter solstice, I was driving with my husband right before sunset, and I pointed out to him how strange the sun looked—almost wrong. It was way over in the south and a pallid lemony color, like I imagine it must look in the Arctic or perhaps from another planet looking toward *its* sun. In winter, it seems the night rules and even the daylight is halfhearted.

And sometimes winter gets dangerous. A few winters ago we had an extreme cold snap. You may remember it if you live far enough north, but actually I think it froze prac-tically everywhere. Here it not only froze, but the tempera-ture, in the deep of the cold, reached a *high* of fifteen below zero. School was canceled and no one went outside unless absolutely necessary. I didn't go out and look for Orion during that time. I remember standing in my warm house, scratching a hole in the ice on the *inside* of the window pane, feeling like I was Laura Ingalls Wilder looking out of the Little House in the Big Woods. I remember thinking, *Stay out too long in this and you could die. Dear Lord, thank you for central heat, and please keep the furnace working.* The storm felt primitive and threatening, as if winter was all-powerful, and all our heat and electricity were but feeble defenses.

Yet this, too, is of God. As the old hymn goes, "Summer and winter, seedtime and harvest—thine own dear pres-ence to cheer and to guide." The grass withers, the flowers fade, but the Word of God endures forever.

Heroes and Stars

My dad's favorite constellation was the Pleiades, a little "west" of Orion. He called these stars his "friends." He had no qualms about standing out in the freezing cold—I have memories of him going outdoors bathrobed and barefoot on bitter winter mornings to feed the birds. (My husband and I were talking the other day about how a lot of people must have "heroic dad memories." One of his was a certain ski trip to Michigan's Upper Peninsula; his dad fixed their trailer generator, barehanded, in subzero temperature. My dad could pinch out a candle flame with his fingers and clean gutters in thunderstorms. Let's see *your* dad top that.)

My dad didn't talk much about spiritual things. I have a feeling he had this whole deep interior life I knew nothing about, but I suspect his idea of heaven would involve the Pleiades more than it would pearly gates. It was also in winter, time of the great constellations, and right before Christmas, when he got sick. For several years thereafter in early December I would feel blue and not very celebratory. It wasn't at all like in the story of the Grinch, when, despite the Grinch having stolen all the toys and roast beast from Who-ville, "Christmas came just the same."

But take the "mas" out of Christmas and here is the point: Christ came just the same. Christ *comes* just the same. Great is his faithfulness.

Time—which is from God, so give him the glory—has healed the wound of losing Dad, sort of. I won't ever feel quite as protected, and I certainly feel a lot older. And even though he wasn't the archetypal family-altar dad I hear some of my friends talk about, I know where he is. I know part of him is in me. And I know I have learned, painfully and sometimes circuitously, through the longing. Besides, I can always look at the Pleiades.

The Fruit of Snow

There's something else about winter I've learned: the more snow, the more green. This is something else I don't quite understand, but it's true. I've seen it.

The winter of 1978–79 was the fiercest ever here-
abouts, which is saying a lot. One mid-January blizzard
dumped four feet of snow on the city. In all, we received
something like a hundred-plus inches of the white stuff.
We've bored our daughter with videotapes, transferred
from home movies, of Mom and Dad dwarfed by eight-foot
drifts. But when all the snow melted—which took until
about April—the earth was as green as I've ever seen it
here. Glowing, almost bluish green, such as I imagine you
see in Ireland. The snow had done something to insulate
and somehow enrich the ground, way down deep.

Something to think about.

Far be it from me to belabor analogies. I don't mean to
say that the more we endure winter's hardships, the better
off we'll be. But if we can understand the winter—including
the winter of the soul—and appreciate its depths, and not
always feel like we have to flee to some warm Club Med of
victory testimonies, we may come that much closer to
knowing the fullness of God.

Another observation, heard from a botanist: Fruits and
vegetables (and mosquitoes) grow biggest at the northern-
most end of their range. Maybe because the fruit has more
to overcome.

"Hi, God!"

Cold. Struggle. Fruit. God gives—and uses—all of it.
"All I have needed, thy hand has provided." Winter melts
into spring and spring, less dramatically, drifts into summer.
The humidity descends and the mosquitoes come back—
but then, so do the fireflies. And sometimes a thundershow-
er is followed by a double rainbow like the one I saw a few
nights ago. Pretty soon it will be the Fourth of July. Then
our vacation! Then sweet-corn season! Remember the

check that *was* in the mail? It came—and went. Spent much of it on airfare. Boy, give the poor a little money and see what happens.

Why am I thinking about all this now, seasons and struggle? I guess because I'm continually amazed by God's constancy, how he brings us through, sometimes in spite of ourselves; how sometimes it's a signal gift just to wake up in the morning and say, "Hi, God! Here I am! There *you* are!"

Wasn't it the Christian mystic Julian of Norwich who said, "All shall be well and all shall be well and all manner of things shall be well"?

Yes, they will.

I look at that affirmation and remember that Philip Yancey once talked about how he will write something and then think, *Do I believe that? Do I, the designated Thomas, really believe that all will be well?*

Yes, but only because Jesus has touched me with his wounds, and because I've seen others touched similarly and have wondered at the ways of God, who uses everything.

Back to my friends and their struggles. For one, the friend with the worst trouble, the situation has resolved itself splendidly, even as I've been writing this book. She's coming out of the valley, which has been more like a journey through a dark gorge. I've been with her all the way, and after the worst was past, we were talking, and she said, "I was really surprised at how well things worked out."

"I wasn't," I said.

Great *is* his faithfulness. Great *has been* his faithfulness. Great *will be* his faithfulness. Any way you conjugate it, it works, now and for always.

Praise him!